Challenge
Activities
Blackline Masters

Level 5

McGraw Hill SRA

Columbus, OH

SRAonline.com

 SRA

Copyright © 2008 by SRA/McGraw-Hill.

All rights reserved. The contents, or parts thereof, may be reproduced in print form for non-profit educational use with *Imagine It!* provided such reproductions bear copyright notice, but may not be reproduced in any form for any other purpose without the prior written consent of The McGraw-Hill Companies, Inc., including, but not limited to, network storage or transmission, or broadcast for distance learning. An Open Court Curriculum.

Printed in the United States of America.

Send all inquiries to this address:
SRA/McGraw-Hill
4400 Easton Commons
Columbus, OH 43219-6188

ISBN: 978-0-07-610364-5
MHID: 0-07-610364-1

3 4 5 6 7 8 9 BCH 13 12 11 10 09 08 07

The McGraw·Hill Companies

Unit 1 Heritage

Unit 2 Energy at Work

Unit 3 Making a New Nation

Unit 4 **Our Corner of the Universe**

(5) Unit 5 Going West

Unit 6 Call of Duty

Name _____ **Date** _____

Root Words

Focus Many words contain **root words** that come from languages other than English. For example, *bicycle* and *recycle* both contain the Greek root *cycl,* which means "circle." Knowing the meaning of a root can help you learn the meanings of words that use the root. However, a word's literal meaning is often different from a word's common English meaning.

Apply **Complete the root word activities below. Use a dictionary if you need help.**

1. Write two words that use the root word *serv* meaning "to save or keep." Use each word in an original sentence. _____

_____

_____

_____

_____

2. Write two words that use the root word *serv* meaning "to serve." Use each word in an original sentence. _____

_____

_____

_____

_____

Name _____ **Date** _____

Selection Vocabulary

 **Focus**

propped	edible	lingered	inspired	unjustly
persecuted	logic	apparently	assumed	reality

Apply Choose four words from your list above, and use the words to write four original sentences about your heritage.

_____

_____

_____

_____

_____

_____

_____

_____

_____

_____

_____

_____

Vocabulary • *Challenge Activities*

Name _____ Date _____

Author's Point of View

Focus Writers must decide from whose point of view they will tell a story.

- **First-person point of view** is told through the eyes of a character in the story. First-person narrators use words such as *I, me, we, us, our,* and *my.*

- **Third-person point of view** is told through the eyes of a narrator who is outside the story. Third-person narrators use words such as *he, she, her, them, theirs, his,* and *hers.*

Apply Imagine you are writing a short paragraph about your heritage or describing a family event. On a separate sheet of paper, write two drafts of the story. Write one draft from the first-person point of view and one draft from the third-person point of view.

Name _____ Date _____

Spelling

Focus soliloquy bookkeeper

Apply Write the definitions of the words *soliloquy* and *bookkeeper* below. Then use the words together in one original sentence.

soliloquy _____

_____

bookkeeper _____

_____

Sentence _____

_____

Write two other words that have the root word *sol*, as in the word *soliloquy*. Use a dictionary if you need help. Write a definition for each word.

1. _____

2. _____

Use the words you provided above in an original sentence.

_____

_____

Name _____ Date _____

Common Nouns and Proper Nouns

Focus

Nouns name people, places, or things.

Rule	Example
• A **common noun** is used to name a general, or nonspecific, person, place, or thing.	• teacher, library
• A **proper noun** is capitalized and used to name a particular, or specific, person, place, or thing.	• Ms. Alvarez, Cook County Library

Apply **Fill in the blanks with appropriate nouns.**

_____ was a good day for _____. She got up early

and cleaned her _____. Then she went to the _____ to

play. At lunch, she had _____ and _____ to eat. After

lunch, she read a book about _____. Since the day was

hot, _____ went for a swim in the _____. To end the

day, _____ asked _____ to watch a video with her

family. Her day had been so full that as soon as _____

went to _____ she fell asleep. That night, she dreamed

of going to the _____.

Name _____ **Date** _____

Prefix *tele-*

Focus　The prefix **tele-** means "far." Adding *tele-* to a base word changes its meaning. For example, *vision* is the ability to see; *television* is the device used to see over images broadcast long distances.

Apply　**Brainstorm four words with the prefix *tele-*. Create a sentence with each one that clearly explains the meaning of the word. Use a dictionary if necessary to check definitions.**

Example
Jim was on the telephone for several hours while communicating with his friend in India.

_____

_____

_____

_____

_____

_____

_____

_____

_____

Name _____ Date _____

Selection Vocabulary

Focus Senegal   lavender   delicate   ignores   ship
traders   surrounded   mist   quivers

Apply Tongue twisters use similar-sounding letters in the beginnings and endings of words.

Unique New York

Toy boats

Cheap ship trips

Select three vocabulary words from the Word Bank, and on a separate sheet of paper, create a two- or three-word tongue twister with each word.

Example

The myth of Miss Muffet

The sheik's sixth sheep's sick.

Whistle for the thistle sifter.

Name _____ Date _____

Spelling

Focus   teletypewriter   disaggregate

Apply   Write the definitions of the words on the lines below.
Then use the words together in one original sentence.

teletypewriter _____

_____

disaggregate _____

_____

Sentence _____

_____

Write two additional words not in the spelling list that have
the prefix *dis-*. Write a definition for each word.

1. _____

2. _____

Use the words you provided above in an original sentence.

_____

_____

Name _____ Date _____

Subjects and Predicates

Focus

A **simple sentence** contains only one independent clause with a subject and a predicate.

Rule	Example
• The **subject** is the part of the sentence that tells *who* or *what.*	• **The students** visited a nature preserve.
• The **predicate** is the part of the sentence that describes or tells what the subject does.	• The students **visited a nature preserve.**
• A **simple subject** is a single key noun or pronoun in a simple sentence.	• **The students** visited a nature preserve.
• A **compound subject** has two or more key nouns linked by a conjunction.	• **The students** and their **teacher** visited a nature preserve.
• The predicate in a simple sentence can also be simple or compound.	• The students **visited a nature preserve.** The students **visited a nature preserve and had a picnic.**

Apply

On a separate sheet of paper, write a paragraph describing something that represents your heritage. Make sure to explain its significance. Trade papers with another student. Then, underline the subjects, and circle the predicates on each other's papers.

Name _____   Date _____

Multiple-Meaning Words

Focus Many words have more than one meaning. You will often need to look at context clues to figure out which meaning is being used in a particular sentence.

Apply The underlined words in the sentences are multiple-meaning words. Using context clues, identify the meaning of the underlined word. Then write a sentence using one of the word's alternate meanings and write the definition on the line.

1. Shelly loved the changing of the <u>seasons</u> from summer to fall.

_____

Meaning: _____

2. The human <u>mind</u> is a powerful tool.

_____

Meaning: _____

3. He sounded the <u>alarm</u> to alert the others of danger.

_____

Meaning: _____

4. Marshall will <u>address</u> the audience after dinner.

_____

Meaning: _____

Name _____ Date _____

Selection Vocabulary

Focus
kimono	phonograph	startled	internment	barrack
sweltered	ascend	donned	soloed	enrich

Apply Write four original sentences on the lines below. Each sentence should use two or more of the vocabulary words listed in the box. Make sure your sentences clearly express the meanings of the words.

_____

_____

_____

_____

_____

_____

_____

_____

_____

_____

_____

_____

_____

_____

Name _____ Date _____

Making Inferences

Focus Writers often do not include every detail about a character or an event in the story. Good readers use clues from the text to **make inferences** in order to complete the picture. Use the writer's clues and your own prior knowledge and experiences to get a better understanding of a character or an event.

Apply **Review further "The Dancing Bird of Paradise"** **or another selection you have read. Use both the** information in the text and your personal knowledge to make three inferences about the relationships described in the story. Explain what information led you to make each inference.

Inference 1: _____

Explanation: _____

_____

Inference 2: _____

Explanation: _____

_____

Inference 3: _____

Explanation: _____

_____

Name _____ **Date** _____

Spelling

 **Focus**   endorsement   undistinguished

 **Apply** Write the definitions of *endorsement* and *undistinguished* on the lines below. Then use the words together in one original sentence.

endorsement _____

_____

undistinguished _____

_____

Sentence _____

_____

Write one additional word that has the prefix *en-* and one additional word that has the prefix *un-*. Write a definition for each word.

1. _____

2. _____

Use the words you provided above in an original sentence.

_____

_____

Name _____ Date _____

Adjectives and Adverbs

Focus

Adjectives modify nouns.

Rule	Example
• Adjectives show what kind, how many, and which one.	• **colorful** shirts; **several** children; **that** cupcake
• Proper adjectives, like proper nouns, are always capitalized.	• **French** toast; **Jewish** deli

Adverbs modify verbs, adjectives, and other adverbs.

Rule	Example
• Adverbs show how, when, where, and to what extent.	• walked **slowly**; bowled **yesterday**; jumping **around**; **very** quiet

Apply   **Fill in the blanks with appropriate adjectives or adverbs.**

1. _____ _____ box contains all of my _____ presents.

2. The _____ door creaked as Suzy opened it.

3. Place _____ vegetables in _____ pot.

4. Finally, we reached _____ _____ corner and walked on to our _____ home.

5. Reduce _____ heat, and add _____ cans of _____ tomatoes.

6. The car drove _____ down the driveway.

7. The movie was _____ long and _____ boring.

8. Finding the _____ lost dog took _____ _____ several hours.

Name _____ **Date** _____

Suffix -ant

Focus The suffix **-ant** means "being in a particular state" or "one who does something." For example, adding the suffix -ant to the word *please* changes it to *pleasant,* or "something that pleases."

Apply Work with a partner, and set a time limit of five minutes. Then, write as many words as you can think of that contain the suffix -ant. When the time is up, switch papers with your partner, and compare word lists. On a separate sheet of paper, use each of your partner's words in an original sentence.

-ant

_____

_____

_____

_____

_____

_____

_____

_____

_____

_____

_____

Name _____ Date _____

Selection Vocabulary

Focus

attitude	claim	magnificent	spellbound	civilizations
section	concert	finest	forbidden	trolley

Apply Summarize "From Miss Ida's Porch." Use each vocabulary word at least once in your summary. Trade papers with a partner, and identify the vocabulary words in each other's paper.

_____

_____

_____

_____

_____

_____

_____

_____

_____

_____

_____

Vocabulary • *Challenge Activities*

Name _____ **Date** _____

Spelling

Focus buoyant   specificity

Apply **Write the definition of the word *buoyant.*** _____

_____

List some materials or items you know that would be

buoyant: _____

Now, list some items that you know are not buoyant: _____

_____

Use the word *buoyant* in an original sentence: _____

_____

Write two additional words that have the suffix *-ity* and two additional words that have the suffix *-ant*. Write a definition for each word.

1. _____

2. _____

Use the words you provided above in an original sentence.

_____

_____

Name _____ **Date** _____

Commas

Focus

Commas organize the thoughts and items in a sentence. They show the reader where to pause so that a sentence's meaning can be clearly understood.

Rule	Example
• Use a comma to separate three or more items.	• I eat bananas, apples, and oranges. Triathletes swim, bike, and run.
• Use a comma after long introductory phrases or clauses.	• **After we finished cleaning the house,** my dad and I relaxed.
• Use a comma and a connecting word to join two independent clauses.	• Luiz wants to play chess, **but** Shonda wants to play checkers.
• Use a comma when an interjection is not followed by an exclamation point.	• **Gosh,** I did not know that. **Hi,** Mr. Harris.
• Use a comma before and after an appositive.	• My friend, **Lacy,** is going to Kentucky.

Apply

On a separate sheet of paper, use comma rules in the following examples.

1. Create a heading for a business letter.

2. Create an inside address for a business letter.

3. Use your birthdate in a sentence; include the day of the week, the month, the date of the day, and the year.

4. Use your address in a sentence; include street address, city, state, and zip code.

5. Use the name of a European city and country in a sentence.

Name _____ **Date** _____

Suffixes *-ence* and *-ly*

Focus
- The suffix **-ence** means "state or quality of being." For example, *convenience* means "the quality of being convenient."
- Adding the suffix **-ly** to an adjective will create an adverb. For example, the adjective *slow* becomes the adverb *slowly*.

Apply Work with a partner, and set a time limit of five minutes. Then, write as many words as you can think of that contain each of the suffixes listed below. When the time is up, switch papers with your partner, and compare word lists. On a separate sheet of paper, use each of your partner's words in an original sentence.

-ence

_____

_____

-ly

_____

_____

Name _____ Date _____

Selection Vocabulary

 **Focus**

vast	tilted	withered	inhabit	role
luxury	freighter	sewage	lagoon	fluent

Apply Write four original sentences on the lines below. Each sentence should use two or more of the vocabulary words listed in the box. Make sure your sentences clearly express the meanings of the words.

_____

_____

_____

_____

_____

_____

_____

_____

_____

_____

_____

_____

_____

_____

Vocabulary • *Challenge Activities*

Name _____ **Date** _____

Compare and Contrast

Focus Writers compare and contrast to paint a clearer picture of the people and things they are writing about.

- To **compare** means to tell how things, ideas, events, or characters are alike.

- To **contrast** means to tell how things, ideas, events, or characters are different.

Apply In twenty years, many things in the world and about you will be different. Complete the chart below to show comparisons and contrasts between your life now and what your life may be like twenty years from now.

Life Now	Life in 20 years

Name _____ Date _____

Spelling

Focus courageously   reticence

Apply   **Would it be possible to do something both courageously and with reticence?**

Explain why you think yes or no: _____

_____

_____

Write two synonyms for the word *courageously* and use each in an original sentence: (use a thesaurus if you need help)

_____

_____

_____

_____

Write two synonyms for the word *reticence* and use each in an original sentence: (use a thesaurus if you need help)

_____

_____

_____

_____

On a separate sheet of paper, write about a time when you did something with *reticence.*

Spelling • *Challenge Activities*

Verbs, Verb Phrases, Direct and Indirect Objects

Rule	Example
• **Verbs** are words that show action or express a state of being.	• Malcolm **grew** tomatoes and peppers. Tomorrow **is** the last day of school.
• **Verb phrases** consist of one or more helping verbs used with an action or state-of-being verb.	• I **have picked** a book for my report. She **could see** the deer running.
• **Direct objects** are nouns and pronouns that receive the action of the verb.	• Pilar finished her **homework.** The artist sculpted a **statue.**
• **Indirect objects** are nouns and pronouns for, or to whom something is done.	• Denzel told his **classmates** a joke. We made our **mother** dinner. Kris sent **Ethan** a letter.

Apply **On a separate sheet of paper, complete the activities below. Trade papers with a partner and underline the verbs and objects in each other's sentences.**

1. Write a sentence containing an action verb.

2. Write a sentence containing a state-of-being verb.

3. Write a sentence using a noun as a direct object.

4. Write a sentence using a noun as an indirect object.

5. Write a sentence with a direct object and a prepositional phrase.

Name _____ Date _____

Compound Words

Focus **Compound words** are words formed by combining two or more smaller words and forming one larger word. If you know the smaller words' meanings, you can often figure out the meaning of the compound word.

Apply Working with a partner, set a time limit of five minutes to make as many compound words as possible from the list of words below. Compare lists with another group. On a separate sheet of paper, use each other's compound words in original sentences.

back	look	side
black	out	spin
board	over	take
come	rail	walk
drop	road	ways
hand		

_____

_____

_____

_____

_____

_____

_____

_____

Word Structure • *Challenge Activities*

Name _____ **Date** _____

Selection Vocabulary

Focus

demonstration	retirement	attracted	donors	inefficient
dissolve	insulators	electrocuted	vents	charged

Apply Write four original sentences on the lines below. Each sentence should use two or more of the vocabulary words listed in the Focus box.

_____

_____

_____

_____

_____

_____

_____

_____

_____

_____

_____

_____

_____

_____

_____

Name _____ Date _____

Spelling

Focus inseparable   breakthrough

Apply Identify the base word of *inseparable.* Write as many words not in the spelling list as you can think of that have the base word, and use each word in an original sentence.

_____

_____

_____

_____

_____

_____

Breakthrough is a compound word. Write some other compound words that begin with the word *break* and define each word.

_____

_____

_____

_____

Spelling • *Challenge Activities*

Name _____ Date _____

Action Verbs

Focus
- **Action verbs** express mental or physical actions.
- Action verbs can be the main verbs in verb phrases.
- Action verbs can also be used in dependent clauses.

- I **understand** what you are saying. Emily **studied** for her test.
- Ted has been **thinking** it over.
- I was relieved when Jen **asked** for help. It was cold because someone **opened** a door.

Apply Imagine that a curious, twelve-year-old Ben Franklin has stumbled into a time warp and is transported onto your front porch. He knocks on your door, hoping to get some answers about where he is and about the purpose of all the modern technology. You answer the door . . .

On a separate sheet of paper, write a continuation of this story using action verbs. Trade papers with another student, and underline the action verbs in each other's paper.

Copyright © SRA/McGraw-Hill. Permission is granted to reproduce this page for classroom use.

Name _____ **Date** _____

Word Origins

Focus Recognizing and understanding **word origins** can help you understand new and unfamiliar words. For example, take the word *microscopic*. It contains the Greek root *scop*. This root means "to look at." The prefix *micro-* means "very small." Thus *microscopic* literally means "too small to be seen."

Apply Work together with a partner. Take turns using a dictionary to find the word origin of each of the words below. Then give clues to help your partner determine the language that the word originated from.

1. cashew

2. mammoth

3. loaf

4. ticket

5. zero

6. cafeteria

7. attitude

8. jungle

9. casserole

10. pajamas

Word Structure • *Challenge Activities*

Name _____ Date _____

Selection Vocabulary

Focus

layer	survey	prediction	severe	alert
raging	inspiration	stovepipe	spiraling	opposing

Apply Imagine that you are a meteorologist who has just heard reports of a tornado sighting from a storm chaser. Your job is to report the news to the television audience. On a separate sheet of paper, use the selection vocabulary words to give the weather report about a tornado sighting. Trade papers with a partner, and share weather reports.

Name _____ **Date** _____

Spelling

Focus insignificant   irresponsible

Apply Write two sentences describing something *insignificant.*

_____

_____

_____

_____

Write one additional word that has the prefix *in-* and one word that has the prefix *ir-*. Write a definition for each word.

1. _____

2. _____

Use the words you provided above in an original sentence.

_____

_____

Spelling • *Challenge Activities*

Name _____ **Date** _____

Electronic Technology: Retrieving and Reviewing Information

Focus

- Searching for and retrieving information is much easier because of **electronic technology.** The Internet, online encyclopedias, and electronic library catalogs provide quick access to large amounts of information. Knowing how to choose **key words** for your searches is an important part of using electronic technology.

- Electronic technology also helps you review the things you have written. **Word-processing programs** can check for errors in spelling and grammar. They will not catch every error, though, so you must still proofread your work. For example, homophones and homographs are often overlooked by word-processing programs.

Apply

Research the process and ingredients necessary to create a minitornado. Write the ingredients and the process on a separate sheet of paper.

Name _____ Date _____

Inflectional Ending -*ed*

Focus
- Adding the inflectional ending -*ed* to a verb forms the past tense of that verb.

They **work** from dawn to dusk. They **worked** from dawn to dusk.

- Verbs that end with the inflectional ending -*ed* can also be used as adjectives or participles.

That **baked** apple smells great!

Apply Add the infectional ending -*ed* to each verb listed in the box. Then, write one sentence using the verb as an adjective and one sentence using it as a verb in the past tense.

dissolve	charge	attract	cook

_____

_____

_____

_____

_____

_____

_____

_____

_____

_____

Word Structure • *Challenge Activities*

Name _____ Date _____

Selection Vocabulary

Focus | observe   negative   positive   hypothesis   squinted
crane   electromagnets   practically   conclusions

Apply   Write four original sentences on the lines below. Each sentence should use two or more of the vocabulary words listed in the Focus box.

_____

_____

_____

_____

_____

_____

_____

_____

_____

_____

_____

_____

_____

Name _____ Date _____

Spelling

Focus illiteracy exasperated

Apply Write two additional words that have the prefix *il-*.
Write a definition for each word.

1. _____

2. _____

Provide an antonym of the word *illiteracy* and use it in an
original sentence.

_____

_____

Provide at least two antonyms of the word *exasperated* and
use them in an original sentence.

_____

_____

Provide at least two synonyms of the word *exasperated* and
use them in an original sentence.

_____

_____

Name _____ Date _____

Subject, Object, and Possessive Pronouns

Focus

Rule	Example
• A **subject pronoun** replaces one or more nouns in the subject. *I, you, he, she, it, we,* and *they* are subject pronouns.	• The kids organized a yard sale. **They** organized a yard sale. Salena ran to first base. **She** ran to first base.
• An **object pronoun** replaces one or more nouns in the predicate. *Me, you, her, him, it, us,* and *them* are object pronouns.	• Ishiko came with **me** to the concert. Uncle Tito played with **them.** I gave **her** my notes. Mr. Fox is looking for **you.**
• A **possessive pronoun** shows ownership. *My, your, her, his, our, your, its,* and *their* are used with nouns. *Mine, yours, hers, his, its, ours, yours,* and *theirs* are used alone.	• **Your** sister scored a goal. Therese can have **mine.** This last apple is **yours.**

Apply On a separate sheet of paper, write four sentences about a science fair, art show, or sporting event of which you have been a part. Include each of the four types of pronouns: subject, possessive, direct object, and indirect object pronouns. Trade papers with a partner, and identify the four different types of pronouns in his or her sentences.

Name _____ Date _____

Comparatives and Superlatives

Focus

- A **comparative adjective** or **adverb** compares one person, thing, or action to another.

- A **superlative adjective** or **adverb** compares one person, thing, or action to several others.

- When forming the **comparative,** most longer modifiers must be preceded by the word **more.**

- When forming the **superlative,** most longer modifiers must be preceded by the word **most.**

- I am **taller** now than I was two years ago.

- That is the **prettiest** painting in the museum.

- Tom was **more patient** than Jim.

- Of all the members of her track team, Kyra runs **most quickly.**

Apply Imagine that you are hired to write a commercial for a new wind turbine company called Urban Wind Turbine. They produce miniature wind turbines for energy use in towns and cities. These small turbines mount on roof tops. Their latest version mounts on the roof of cars and recharges the electric motor. Your assignment is to write a three-minute commercial, on a separate sheet of paper, about the new car model turbine (or one of their other products). Use four or more comparative and superlative adjectives and adverbs in your commercial.

Word Structure • *Challenge Activities*

Name _____ Date _____

Selection Vocabulary

Focus

| gusty | propel | revolving doors | fossil fuels | flickering |
| converts | economical | reliable | currents | expands |

Apply

Write three extended metaphors about windmills or wind turbines. Use at least three vocabulary words in each of your metaphors.

_____

_____

_____

_____

_____

_____

_____

_____

_____

_____

_____

_____

_____

_____

Name _____ Date _____

Cause and Effect

Focus

When one event causes another to happen, the events have a **cause-and-effect relationship.**

- A **cause** is the reason that an event happens.

- An **effect** is the result of a cause.

- Writers use words such as *because, since, therefore,* and *so* to show the reader that a cause-and-effect relationship has taken place.

Apply

Now write two cause-and-effect riddles of your own on a separate sheet of paper.

Many jokes rely on a cause-and-effect relationship for their humor. For example:

Effects

1. What can you break by saying it?

2. Why did the hat and the tie say "Good-bye"?

3. Why is "smiles" the longest word in the dictionary?

Causes

1. Silence

2. Because one went on ahead and the other hung around.

3. Because there is a "mile" between each s.

Name _____ Date _____

Spelling

Focus reauthorize   anachronism

Apply Write the definition of *anachronism* on the lines below. Then, use the word *anachronism* in an original sentence with the word *reauthorize*.

_____

_____

_____

_____

Write at least two additional words that have the same Greek root as the word *anachronism*. Write a definition for each word.

1. _____

_____

2. _____

_____

Write at least two additional words that have the prefix *re-*. Write a definition for each word.

1. _____

_____

2. _____

Name _____   **Date** _____

Regular and Irregular Plurals

Focus

Rule	Example
• For words that end in a consonant and *y*, change the *y* to *i* and then add *-es*.	• baby, babies fly, flies
• For some words that end in *f* or *fe*, change the *f* or *fe* to *v* and add *-es*.	• loaf, loaves shelf, shelves
• For words that end in a consonant and *o*, add either *-s* or *-es*. You must use a dictionary to determine which is correct.	• mango, mangos potato, potatoes rhino, rhinos
• For some words, the plural form is a different word.	• tooth, teeth child, children
• For some words, the singular and plural forms are the same.	• deer, deer sheep, sheep

Apply For each of the rules, write two original sentences on a separate sheet of paper using the correct plural form of a word that follows the following rules.

1. To form the plural of most nouns, add *-s* or *-es*.

2. For nouns ending with *s, z, ch, sh,* or *x*, add *-es*.

3. If a noun ends in a consonant and *y,* change the *y* to an *i* and add *-es*.

4. If a noun ends in *f* or *fe,* change the *f* to a *v* and add *-es or s*.

Grammar, Usage, and Mechanics • *Challenge Activities*

Name _____   Date _____

Words with Latin Roots

Focus Identifying and understanding **Latin roots** can help you define difficult words. When you know the meanings of a word's root or roots, you can sometimes figure out the word's general meaning.

Apply Working with a partner, in five minutes write as many words as you can that contain each Latin root.

1. *cap,* meaning "head"

_____

_____

2. *form,* meaning "shape"

_____

_____

3. *miss,* meaning "send"

_____

_____

4. *dic,* meaning "say"

_____

_____

5. *hosp,* meaning "guest"

_____

_____

Name _____ Date _____

Selection Vocabulary

ecosystem food chain food web   ridges   algae
absorbs   diet   omnivores predators scavenger

Imagine that you are the tour guide on a Wild Animal
Park Photo Safari. Use at least five of the selection
vocabulary words to write your monologue.

_____

_____

_____

_____

_____

_____

_____

_____

_____

_____

_____

_____

_____

_____

_____

Vocabulary • *Challenge Activities*

Name _____ Date _____

Classify and Categorize

Focus
Classifying and categorizing are ways of organizing information. They can help you better understand and remember what you have read.

- **Classifying** is identifying the similarities that objects, characters, or events have in common with each other, and then grouping them by their similarities.

- **Categorizing** is the act of organizing the objects, characters, or events into groups, or categories.

Apply
From your experience, you have probably learned that it is easier to classify things than it is to classify ideas. Because ideas are abstract and can be interpreted in different ways, it is sometimes difficult to assign them to specific categories. On a separate sheet of paper, create a chart of some of your ideas about the unit theme Energy at Work. Your category headings will depend on the ideas you list.

Name _____ Date _____

Spelling

Focus nonexistent   jurisprudence

Apply Write the definitions of the words *nonexistent* and *jurisprudence* below. Then use the words together in one original sentence.

nonexistent _____

_____

jurisprudence _____

_____

Sentence _____

_____

Write two other words not in the spelling list that have the prefix *non-*. Write a definition for each word.

1. _____

2. _____

Use the words you provided above in an original sentence.

_____

_____

Spelling • *Challenge Activities*

Name _____ Date _____

Conjunctions

Focus
- A **conjunction** is a word that connects words or groups of words. A **coordinating conjunction** joins words or groups of words that are equally important in a sentence. Coordinating conjunctions include *and, but, or, nor, yet,* and *for.*
- **Subordinating conjunctions** connect two clauses where one clause is grammatically dependent on the other. Some subordinating conjunctions include *after, although, before, if, so* and *when.*

Apply **Combine and rewrite these sentences using the following coordinating conjunctions:** *and, but, or, yet, nor, for.* **Use a different conjunction for each one.**

1. Josh sold tickets. Brandon ran the projector.

_____

2. Carol caught the ball. Then, she dropped it.

_____

Combine and rewrite these sentences using the following subordinating conjunctions: *after, although, before, if, so, when, while.* **Use a different conjunction for each one.**

3. We got up early. The sun came over the hill.

_____

_____

4. Dad was washing the car. Jacob was mowing the lawn.

_____

_____

Name _____ Date _____

Irregular Verbs

Focus The rule for forming the past tense of most verbs is to add -ed. **Irregular verbs** do not follow this rule. Instead, you must learn both the present tense and the past tense forms of each verb.

Apply Imagine that you lived during the time of the American Revolution. Use your knowledge of the time period to write a short paragraph on a separate sheet of paper using the present tense of some of the irregular verbs listed below. Or imagine that you are a historian looking back on the time of the American Revolution. Write your paragraph using the past tense of some of the irregular verbs listed below. Ask your teacher about sharing your finished paragraph with the class.

give	gave
be	been
tell	told
am	was
eat	ate
go	went
say	said

Word Structure • *Challenge Activities*

Name _____ **Date** _____

Selection Vocabulary

Focus

colonies	loyal	settlers	protest
liberty	militia	necessities	pamphlets
published	discharge		

Apply Choose six of the vocabulary words above. In your own words, write a sentence defining each word. Then, check your definition against the glossary in the back of the *Student Reader.*

1. _____

_____

2. _____

_____

3. _____

_____

4. _____

_____

5. _____

_____

6. _____

_____

Name _____ Date _____

Cause and Effect

Focus
When one event causes another to happen, the events have a **cause-and-effect** relationship.

- A **cause** is the reason that an event happens.
- An **effect** is the result of a cause.
- Writers use words such as *because, since, therefore,* and *so* to show the reader that a cause-and-effect relationship has taken place.

Apply
On a separate sheet of paper, create a cause-and-effect web like the one below. Use this web to list at least four causes of the Revolutionary War. Then, extend the web beyond the war and record at least three effects the Revolutionary War had on the colonists. Verify that all of your effects were actual results of the causes.

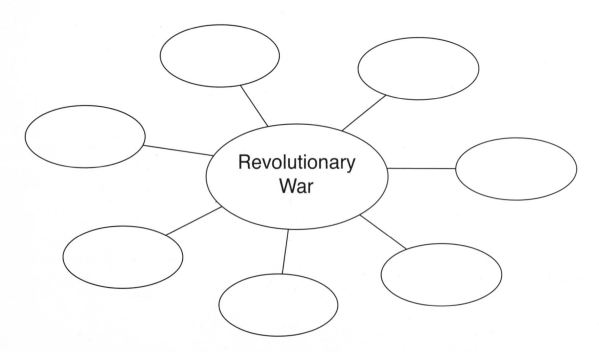

Name _____ Date _____

Spelling

Focus   consolidated   midday

Apply   Write as many words as you can think of using the letters in the word *consolidated.* Use at least two of your words in one original sentence.

_____

_____

_____

_____

Write the definitions of the words *consolidated* and *midday* below. Then use the words together in one original sentence.

consolidated _____

_____

_____

midday _____

_____

_____

Sentence _____

_____

Name _____   **Date** _____

Comparative and Superlative Adjectives and Adverbs

Focus

- A **comparative** adjective or adverb compares one person, thing, or action with another.

- A **superlative** adjective or adverb compares one person, thing, or action with several others.

Apply   Alan, Jack, and Marcus are all brothers who share some interests, but are also different in many ways. On a separate sheet of paper, write a paragraph about these brothers using comparative and superlative adjectives and adverbs from the box below to describe their talents in relation to one another. Use your imagination.

better	best	quicker	more quietly	larger

Name _____ **Date** _____

Homophones

Focus **Homophones** are words that sound the same but have different spellings and meanings. Homophones are challenging because you have to memorize which spelling goes with which definition.

Apply **On a separate sheet of paper, write two sentences using the homophones provided. Make sure you use each word correctly, according to its definition.**

1. clothes, close

2. ant, aunt

3. band, banned

4. doe, dough

5. heal, heel

6. missed, mist

Name _____ **Date** _____

Selection Vocabulary

aloft	muffled	magnified	mount
gleam	ledge	sentinel	weathercock
assigned	spread		

Apply Write four original sentences using the vocabulary words listed in the box. Each sentence should contain at least two vocabulary words.

_____

_____

_____

_____

_____

_____

_____

_____

_____

_____

_____

Vocabulary • *Challenge Activities*

Name _____ Date _____

Spelling

Focus thoughtless   passageway

Apply Write two additional words not in the spelling list that have the suffix *-less.* Write a definition for each word.

1. _____

2. _____

List some antonyms for the word *thoughtless.* _____

_____

List some synonyms for the word *thoughtless.* _____

_____

Define *passageway* and use it in an original sentence.

_____

_____

_____

_____

Name _____ **Date** _____

Prepositional Phrases

Focus

A **preposition** relates a noun or pronoun to another word in the sentence. A **prepositional phrase** is a group of words that begins with a preposition and ends with a noun or pronoun which is the object of the preposition. A prepositional phrase can function as an adjective or an adverb.

Apply

On a separate sheet of paper, write two poems using the subjects "Snow" for one and "The Sun" for the other. Use at least one prepositional phrase in each line.

Example:

Rain

Rain on the green grass,
And rain on the tree,
Rain on the housetop,
But not on me.

Name _____ Date _____

Base Word Families

Focus A **base word** can take many forms when different prefixes, suffixes, and roots are added to it. The words in a base word family can be nouns, verbs, adjectives, or adverbs. When you know the meaning of the base word, you can begin to find the meanings of the words in the base word family.

Apply **Find four words that share the same base words as the words in the box below. Write sentences that use context clues to show the meaning of each word.**

Example: I took many precautions to ensure that I was not burned by the fire.

Base Word	Definition
civil	relating to the people of a country
caution	a warning about danger
arm	weaponry, to supply with weaponry
obey	to follow commands

_____

_____

_____

_____

_____

Name _____ Date _____

Selection Vocabulary

Focus

looting	commander	invaders	prompt
civilians	revealing	idle	precautions
lessen	portrait		

Apply Use the vocabulary words from Lesson 3 to create six word scrambles that include clues about each word's definition. Exchange papers with a partner and solve each other's scrambles.

Example: Stealing things: tolniog   Answer: looting

_____

_____

_____

_____

_____

_____

_____

_____

_____

_____

_____

_____

_____

Name _____ Date _____

Drawing Conclusions

Focus **Drawing conclusions** means putting information together to make a statement about a character or event in a story. While a conclusion may not be directly stated in the text, it should be supported by information in the story.

Apply **Pick a person, place, or thing about which you know several interesting facts. On the lines below, write a descriptive paragraph about it without stating its name. Trade papers with a partner and draw a conclusion about what their paragraph describes.**

Example: She works in any weather. She works every day but Sunday. She knows when people move away and when they leave town for long vacations. Her hands are dry from handling a lot of paper and envelopes.

Answer: mail carrier

_____

_____

_____

_____

_____

_____

_____

_____

_____

_____

Name _____ Date _____

Spelling

 **Focus**   embezzlement   justifiable

 **Apply**   Write the definitions of the words *embezzlement* and *justifiable* below. Then use the words together in one original sentence.

embezzlement _____

_____

_____

justifiable _____

_____

_____

Sentence _____

_____

Write at least two additional words that have the suffix *-ment* and two words that have the suffix *-able*. On a separate sheet of paper, write a definition for each word.

_____

_____

Name _____ Date _____

Electronic Technology: Creating Text

Focus Creating text is faster and easier to do once you have learned how to use electronic technology. Many schools and libraries have computers with word-processing programs available to the public.

Apply Imagine that you are writing a word-processing instruction manual. Explain how to create text using a word-processing program, making sure that your instructions are clear and accurate. Trade papers with another student and follow the instruction manual to create a document.

_____

_____

_____

_____

_____

_____

_____

_____

_____

_____

_____

Name _____   Date _____

Plurals

Focus   The **plural** of many words is formed by adding -s or -es.

Rule	Example
• For words that end in a consonant and *y,* change the *y* to *i* and add -es.	• cherry, cherries colony, colonies
• For words that end in a vowel and *y,* just add -s.	• key, keys
• For some words that end in *f* or *fe* change the *f* or *fe* to *v* and add -es.	• wife, wives calf, calves
• For words that end in a consonant and *o,* you add -es.	• potato, potatoes
• For words that end in *o* preceded by a vowel, just add -s.	• radio, radios
• For words that end in *s, z, ch, sh,* or *x,* just add -es.	• scratch, scratches

tomato	tax	face	leaf
belief	turkey	radio	city

Apply   For every word above, find one more word that follows the same pattern in forming the plural.
On a separate sheet of paper, write both the singular and plural forms of these words.

Word Structure • *Challenge Activities*

Name _____ **Date** _____

Selection Vocabulary

Focus

character	allegiance	central	concern
delegates	league	contribute	eavesdroppers
accomplishment	rumors		

Apply   Based on what you learned in Unit 3, write a short descriptive paragraph about George Washington and his contributions to the founding of our country. Your paragraph should include at least five vocabulary words from the box above. When you finish your paragraph, share it with the class.

_____

_____

_____

_____

_____

_____

_____

_____

_____

_____

_____

Name _____ **Date** _____

Spelling

Focus | condescend | deteriorating

Apply | Write the definitions of the words *condescend* and *deteriorating* below. Then use the words together in one original sentence.

condescend _____

_____

_____

deteriorating _____

_____

_____

Sentence _____

_____

_____

Spelling • *Challenge Activities*

Name _____ **Date** _____

Capitalization

Focus
- Capitalize the specific names of people and places.
- Capitalize the titles of books, movies, magazines, and newspapers.
- Capitalize the first word in a sentence and the first word in a direct quotation.
- Capitalize the names of religions, languages, ethnic backgrounds, and abbreviations.

Apply On the lines below, write a brief summary of the **Virginia Plan, as described on page 310 of "Shh! We're Writing the Constitution." In your summary, do not capitalize any words. Then exchange papers with a partner and correct the capitalization errors that you find.**

_____

_____

_____

_____

_____

_____

_____

_____

_____

_____

Name _____ Date _____

Comparative and Superlative Adjectives and Adverbs

Focus

Rule	**Example**
• A **comparative adjective or adverb** compares one person, thing, or action to another.	• I am *taller* now than I was two years ago.
• A **superlative adjective or adverb** compares one person, thing, or action to several others.	• That is the *prettiest* painting in the museum.
• When forming the comparative, some words must be preceded by the word *more*.	• Tom was *more patient* than Jim.
• When forming the superlative, some words must be preceded by the word *most*.	• Of all the members of her track team, Kyra runs *most quickly*.

Apply Work with a partner to write sentences on a separate sheet of paper using the following guidelines to compare and contrast your similarities and differences. Use comparative and superlative adjectives and adverbs in all of your sentences.

1. Compare your height.

2. Compare your two heights with another person's height.

3. Compare your hair color.

4. Compare your classroom decorations with another classroom in your school.

Word Structure • *Challenge Activities*

Name _____ Date _____

Selection Vocabulary

Focus

utter	declarations	draft	rights
bombarded	retreat	debate	exposing
composition	treason		

Apply Write four original sentences using the vocabulary words listed in the box. Each sentence should contain at least two vocabulary words. Make sure your sentences clearly express the meanings of the words.

_____

_____

_____

_____

_____

_____

_____

_____

_____

_____

Name _____ Date _____

Main Idea and Details

Focus Authors organize their writing into a **main idea** supported by **details.**

- A main idea should be clear and focused.
- A main idea should have supporting details. Details provide additional information about the main idea.

Apply Using the information you learned about Thomas Jefferson from "Give Me Liberty!" write a short paragraph that includes several details to support the following main idea: Thomas Jefferson was ideally suited to write the first draft of the Declaration of Independence. In your paragraph, include at least one piece of information that does not fit with the main idea. Then exchange papers with a partner, and identify the information that does not fit with the main idea.

_____

_____

_____

_____

_____

_____

_____

_____

Comprehension Skill • *Challenge Activities*

Name _____ Date _____

Spelling

**Focus** | calamity | catastrophe

Apply | Write the definitions of the words *calamity* and *catastrophe* below. Then, use the words together in one original sentence.

calamity _____

_____

_____

catastrophe _____

_____

_____

Sentence _____

_____

_____

List some words that are synonyms for *calamity*.

_____

_____

List some words that are antonyms for *calamity*.

_____

_____

Name _____ Date _____

Electronic Technology: Revising Text

Focus Today, most people write using word-processing programs. Revising a text is faster and easier to do once you have learned how to use electronic technology. Many schools and libraries have computers with word-processing programs available to the public.

Apply **Imagine that it is your job to edit the instruction manual for using electronic technology to edit word-processing documents. Read the instructions below, and rewrite them on another sheet of paper with the editing corrections you think are necessary. Use a word-processing program on a computer, if available.**

Cuting and pastin

The cut and paste icons word, sentence, paragraph, allow you to move a or even a whole document from place one to another. First, seletc the test you wanna move. click the cut icon (a pare of scissors). Next, place you want the text to be move the pointer to the. Then clik the cutin and plastering icons <an clip bord//an the tex wil B mowed to the knew locasion.

Name _____ Date _____

Greek Roots

Focus **Greek roots** are common in the English language. Identifying and understanding Greek roots can help you define difficult and unfamiliar words. When you know the meanings of a word's root or roots, you can sometimes figure out the word's general meaning.

Apply **Write one word that uses each Greek root below, and write its definition on the line.**

1. auto

_____

2. bio

_____

3. cycl

_____

4. geo

_____

5. gram

_____

6. mech

_____

7. scop

_____

Name _____ Date _____

Selection Vocabulary

Focus

infinity	disks	clusters	bulges	cosmic
spokes	galaxy	spiral	detect	collapse

Apply The following selection vocabulary words can be used as different parts of speech: *clusters*-noun, verb; *bulges*-noun, verb; *spiral*-noun, verb, adjective; *collapse*-noun, verb; *gusts*-noun, verb. Write five original sentences using at least two of the five words.

_____

_____

_____

_____

_____

_____

_____

_____

_____

_____

Name _____ Date _____

Classify and Categorize

Focus Classifying and categorizing are ways of organizing information. They can help you better understand and remember what you read.

- **Classifying** is identifying the similarities that objects, characters, or events have in common with each other, and then grouping them by their similarities.

- **Categorizing** is the act of organizing the objects, characters, or events into groups, or categories.

Apply Use a card or computer catalog to conduct a search on the key word *stars*. Classify the information that your search yields into categories. For example, you will likely have a category for information on *stars in the sky* and another for information on *movie stars*. List these and other categories you find. Then, think of ways to further classify information in the categories. For example, stars can be further classified as red giants, white dwarfs, or pulsar.

Finally, create a chart that illustrates that you classified and categorized the information you found. Draw your chart on a separate sheet of paper.

Name _____ Date _____

Spelling

Focus pseudonym   astronomical

Apply **Write the definition of *pseudonym* on the lines below. Then, use the word *pseudonym* in an original sentence.**

_____

_____

_____

_____

Write the meaning of the prefix *pseudo-* and write the literal definition of the word *pseudonym*.

_____

_____

_____

Write the definition of *astronomical* on the lines below. Then, use the word *astronomical* in an original sentence.

_____

_____

_____

_____

Name _____ Date _____

Demonstrative Pronouns

Focus A pronoun is a word that takes the place of one or more nouns. A **demonstrative pronoun** points out or indicates a specific person, place, thing, or idea. *This, these, that,* and *those* are demonstrative pronouns.

Apply On a separate sheet of paper, write four original sentences that contain a person, place, thing, or idea that could be replaced by a demonstrative pronoun. Trade papers with a partner. Rewrite the sentences replacing the appropriate word or words with a demonstrative pronoun.

Example: Her mom asked her to pick up the pencils that were on the floor.

Her mom asked her to pick those up.

Name _____ Date _____

Multiple-Meaning Words

Focus **Multiple-meaning words** are words that are spelled the same and have the same word origins but have more than one meaning. You will often need to look at context clues to figure out which meaning is being used in a particular sentence.

Apply The underlined words in the sentences are verbs. They can also be used as nouns with different meanings. Write a sentence using the word as a noun with a different meaning. Then write the meaning of the word on the line.

1. Sheldon did not <u>break</u> his leg when he went skating.

_____

_____

Meaning: _____

2. I did not want to <u>peer</u> too closely into the microscope.

_____

_____

Meaning: _____

3. I <u>will</u> go to the zoo on Sunday.

_____

_____

Meaning: _____

Word Structure • *Challenge Activities*

Name _____ **Date** _____

Selection Vocabulary

Focus

stargazers	observatories	archaeology	abandoned	devised
dramatic	calculations	vertical	bull's-eye	solar

Apply Choose six of the vocabulary words above. In your own words, write a sentence defining each word. Then, check your definition against the glossary in the back of the *Student Reader.*

1. _____

_____

2. _____

_____

3. _____

_____

4. _____

_____

5. _____

_____

6. _____

_____

Name _____ **Date** _____

Compare and Contrast

Writers compare and contrast to paint a clearer picture of the people and things they are writing about.

- To **compare** means to tell how things, ideas, events, or characters are alike.

- To **contrast** means to tell how things, ideas, events, or characters are different.

Review the selection "Circles, Squares, and Daggers." Compare and contrast the Native American observatories described in the selection with modern observatories.

_____

_____

_____

_____

_____

_____

_____

_____

_____

_____

_____

_____

      Comprehension Skill • *Challenge Activities*

Name _____ **Date** _____

Spelling

Focus   insurrection   restitution

Apply   **Write the definitions of *insurrection* and *restitution* on the lines below. Then use the words together in one original sentence.**

insurrection

_____

_____

restitution

_____

_____

Sentence

_____

_____

Write two additional words that have the suffix *-tion/-ion*. Write a definition for each word.

1. _____

2. _____

Name _____ **Date** _____

Formatting

Focus

Formatting is how text is organized and presented on a printed page. The format can change depending on what you write and on your audience. For example, a letter of request would not be formatted in the same way as a research report would be.

Apply

Select the appropriate components from the box, and construct a letter of request on a separate sheet of paper or in a word-processing program. Not all of the components in the box are part of a business letter. Label each component of your letter. Be sure to use the appropriate punctuation and format.

Closing	Signature	Body
Salutation	Heading	Inside Address
Headline	Byline	Title
Introduction	Conclusion	

Name _____ **Date** _____

Word Origins

Focus Recognizing and understanding **word origins** can help you understand new and unfamiliar words. For example, take the word *microscopic.* It contains the Greek root *scop.* This root means "to look at." The prefix *micro-* means "very small." Put the pieces together, and you discover that *microscopic* means "too small to be seen."

Apply **Complete the exercise to familiarize yourself with Latin roots. Use a dictionary to check your predictions.**

Port **is a Latin root. Write two words that use this root.**

1. _____

2. _____

What do you think the root *port* means? _____

Liber **is a Latin root. Write two words that use this root.**

1. _____

2. _____

What do you think the root *liber* means? _____

Sens **is a Latin root. Write two words that use this root.**

1. _____

2. _____

What do you think the root *sens* means? _____

Name _____ Date _____

Selection Vocabulary

Focus

impact	deflated	analyze	texture	hospitable
microscopic	harsh	haze	accumulate	pressure

Apply Use the vocabulary words from Lesson 3 to create five word scrambles that include clues about each word's definition. Exchange papers with a partner, and solve each other's scrambles.

Example: Mist   zahe   Answer: *haze*

_____

_____

_____

_____

_____

_____

_____

_____

_____

_____

_____

Vocabulary • *Challenge Activities*

Name _____ **Date** _____

Spelling

Focus interplanetary   rhythmically

Apply Write the base word of *interplanetary*. _____

Write the definition of *interplanetary*.

_____

_____

Provide two other words that are in the same base word family. Use each word in an original sentence.

_____

_____

_____

_____

Provide the base word of *rhythmically*. _____

Write the definition of *rhythmically* and use it in an original sentence.

_____

_____

_____

_____

Name _____ Date _____

Independent and Dependent Clauses

Focus A **clause** is a group of words that has a subject and a verb.

- An **independent clause** can stand alone as a sentence.

- A **dependent clause** has a subject and a verb, but it cannot stand alone as a sentence.

- I found the book in the fiction section.

- I found the book *that Julie needed for school* in the fiction section.

Apply **On a separate sheet of paper, write a sentence using one of the independent clauses and one of the dependent clauses in the box below. Make the sentence more interesting by adding another dependent clause of your own.**

Independent Clauses	Dependent Clauses
he peered out of the small window	when the spacecraft landed on Mars
the harsh landscape did not look habitable	the haze cleared to reveal
his job was to analyze the microscopic particles	as a geologist, she was
she stepped onto the surface	as the clock ticked away
they could not believe their good fortune	the impact of the spacecraft caused

Synonyms and Antonyms

Focus

Antonyms are words with opposite, or nearly opposite, meanings. An antonym for *empty* is *full,* and an antonym for *dull* is *exciting.*

Synonyms are words with the same, or nearly the same, meanings. A synonym for *exciting* is *thrilling.*

Apply

Write an antonym (A) or a synonym (S) for the word in parentheses that best fits the sentence.

1. The army was forced to _____ after its victory. (advance) (A)

2. When my model collapsed next to Jenny's, I realized my model was _____ to hers. (superior) (A)

3. As my eyes scanned the page _____, I noticed the words were bigger at the top than at the bottom. (horizontally) (A)

4. I _____ my papers before writing my final draft. (scattered) (A)

5. Although my vacation was _____, I enjoyed it tremendously. (lengthy) (A)

6. The directions for assembling the computer were too _____. (simple) (A)

7. Her way of living _____ enabled her to take a vacation once a year. (extravagantly) (A)

8. Nitesh was _____ about performing in the play. (confident) (S)

9. Jim always followed his _____ sports team, no matter how poorly they performed. (favorite) (S)

10. She was _____ to see a birthday had been planned. (surprised) (S)

Name _____ Date _____

Selection Vocabulary

Focus

module	bulky	focused	thrust	hatch
tranquility	depressed	awe	sensations	mankind

Apply   On the lines below, write a short paragraph about a journey into space. Use your knowledge of space missions from "Apollo 11: First Moon Landing" as a guide. Your paragraph should contain at least five of the vocabulary words from the box above.

_____

_____

_____

_____

_____

_____

_____

_____

_____

_____

_____

_____

                   Vocabulary • *Challenge Activities*

Name _____ Date _____

Drawing Conclusions

Focus Writers cannot describe every detail about people or events in a story. Good readers draw conclusions using the information they have been given. **Drawing conclusions** means using the information in the text to make a statement about a person or event. The conclusion is not stated by the author, but the information in the text supports it.

Apply When investigating a topic, researchers use multiple sources to answer questions they have raised about the topic. Think of a question you have that relates to the theme Our Corner of the Universe. This question may stem from the selection "Apollo 11: First Moon Landing" or from another source you have read on the unit theme. Use information from two or more sources to draw a conclusion that answers your question. Then, on a separate sheet of paper, write a paragraph using your conclusion as the topic sentence. Provide at least three clues from your sources to support your conclusion.

Name _____ Date _____

Spelling

Focus extraordinary   fantastic

Apply Write the definitions of *extraordinary* and *fantastic* on the lines below. Then, use the words together in one original sentence.

extraordinary _____

_____

_____

fantastic _____

_____

_____

Sentence _____

_____

_____

Write as many synonyms as you can think of for the word *extraordinary*.

_____

_____

_____

Name _____ Date _____

Apostrophes

Focus **Apostrophes** can be used to show possession.

A **contraction** is formed by combining two words and omitting one or more letters. An apostrophe replaces the missing letters.

Apply **Write a sentence for each word below. Be sure to note whether the word is a possessive, a contraction, or both. Once you have completed your sentences, trade papers with a partner, and check each other's work.**

1. It's _____

_____

2. He'd _____

_____

3. Jamal's _____

_____

4. They're _____

_____

5. Their _____

_____

Name _____ Date _____

Homographs

Focus **Homographs** are words that are spelled exactly the same but have different meanings, different origins, and sometimes different pronunciations. Some homographs are pronounced differently because the stress is placed on different syllables.

Apply **The following pairs of words are homographs. Write a definition for each word as a noun and as a verb. Then use each in a sentence.**

1. console (noun) _____

Sentence: _____

2. console (verb) _____

Sentence: _____

3. rose (noun) _____

Sentence: _____

4. rose (verb) _____

Sentence: _____

5. dove (noun) _____

Sentence: _____

6. dove (verb) _____

Sentence: _____

Name _____ Date _____

Selection Vocabulary

Focus

transferring	responsibilities	confidence
discouraged	application	processes
eclipse	precise	varies
advance		

Apply

Write four sentences using two or more of the vocabulary words listed in the box. Make sure your sentences clearly express the meanings of the words.

_____

_____

_____

_____

_____

_____

_____

_____

_____

_____

_____

_____

Challenge Activities • Vocabulary

Name _____ Date _____

Spelling

Focus   facsimile   vacuum

Apply   Write the definition of *vacuum* on the lines below.
Write two different definitions for the word.

_____

_____

_____

_____

**Use each meaning that you provided for the word
vacuum in an original sentence.**

1. _____

_____

2. _____

_____

Write the definition of *facsimile* on the lines below.

_____

_____

What does the root word *fac* mean? _____

Spelling • *Challenge Activities*

Name _____ Date _____

Subject and Verb Agreement

Focus The verb form used in a sentence must agree with the subject in number. The present-tense verb form used is determined by whether the subject of a sentence is singular or plural.

- Add -s or -es to present tense verbs when they are singular.

- Do not add -s or -es to present tense verbs when they are plural or used with *I* or *you.*

- A compound subject—two or more subjects connected by *and*— uses the plural form of the verb.

Apply **Read the paragraph aloud. Cross out the incorrect verbs, and write the corrections needed for subject and verb agreement above them.**

NASA radar were used to locate a lost plane that crash in

the mountains of Montana. This radar detect things through

clouds, leaves, brush, and even darkness. When weather,

trees, and steep mountains makes it difficult to find downed

planes, NASA's radar could saves lives. Scientists is working

on ways to make this technology available for immediate

search and rescue missions.

Name _____   Date _____

Words with Latin Roots

Focus Identifying and understanding **Latin roots** can help you define difficult and unfamiliar words. When you know the meaning of a root, you can figure out the meanings of many words that contain that root.

Apply The word *spirit* can be found throughout the selection "Buffalo Hunt." It contains the Latin root *spir,* meaning "to breathe." Write down other words that use the Latin root *spir.* Write the literal and actual definitions of each word. On a separate sheet of paper, use each word in an original sentence. Use a dictionary if you need help.

_____

_____

_____

_____

_____

_____

_____

_____

_____

Name _____ Date _____

Selection Vocabulary

Focus

| legends | sacred | stampede | banners | lurking |
| procession | elders | cow | ladles | pitched |

Apply Write a descriptive paragraph using at least five of the selection vocabulary words listed in the Focus box. Trade descriptions with a classmate, and try to determine what is being described.

_____

_____

_____

_____

_____

_____

_____

_____

_____

_____

_____

_____

_____

_____

Name _____ Date _____

Spelling

Focus   terrestrial   veracity

Apply   **Identify the root word in *terrestrial* and define it.**

_____

_____

Identify the root word in *veracity* and define it.

_____

_____

Write the definitions of the words *terrestrial* and *veracity* below. Then, use the words together in one original sentence.

terrestrial _____

_____

_____

veracity _____

_____

_____

Sentence _____

_____

Copyright © SRA/McGraw-Hill. Permission is granted to reproduce this page for classroom use.

       Spelling · *Challenge Activities*

Name _____ **Date** _____

Verb Tense and Sentence Tense

Focus

- **Present tense** = action happening now or on a regular basis
- **Past tense** = action that has already happened
- **Future tense** = action that will happen

- I **feel** a mosquito on my neck. Sean **feels** relief whenever he finishes a math test.
- Jamie **felt** bad when her favorite sports team **lost.**
- John **will feel** relaxed as soon the test is over.

Apply

use	provide
supply	form

On a separate sheet of paper, use the verbs from "Buffalo Hunt" listed in the box to write original sentences for each verb tense. Make sure each sentence clearly conveys meaning and tense. Also, make sure each word is represented in each tense.

Name _____ Date _____

Suffix -*ent*

The suffix -*ent* means "having the quality of." When it is added to a root word, it usually forms an adjective.

Use each word with the suffix -*ent* in the box in an original sentence. The sentence should clearly express the meaning of the chosen word.

urgent	repellent	opponent
evident	eloquent	incoherent

_____

_____

_____

_____

_____

_____

_____

_____

_____

_____

_____

Word Structure • *Challenge Activities*

Name _____ **Date** _____

Selection Vocabulary

Focus

immigrants	endure	rationed	burden	squat
theory	boast	registered	investment	raggedy

Apply Write a clue for five of the selection vocabulary words listed in the Focus box. Use one or two sentences to describe each of the five words. Trade papers with another student, and try to determine which words are being described.

_____

_____

_____

_____

_____

_____

_____

_____

_____

_____

_____

_____

_____

_____

Name _____ Date _____

Sequence

Focus When writers tell a story or explain a process, they must express the **sequence** in which events occur.

Sequence is indicated by time and order words.

- Words such as *earlier, later, now, then, morning, day, evening,* and *night* indicate time.

- Words such as *first, second, last, following, next, after, during,* and *finally* indicate order.

Apply Think of all the words and phrases you know that indicate a time of day, an amount of time, or an order in which events take place. On a separate sheet of paper, write a poem about time using those words. You might describe what it feels like to have to wait for something, or you might describe how time seems to pass slowly or quickly in different situations. Remember to use time and order words or phrases in your poem.

Comprehension Skill • *Challenge Activities*

Name _____ Date _____

Spelling

Focus   contaminant   benevolent

Apply   Write at least two additional words that have the suffix *-ant.* Write a definition for each word.

1. _____

_____

2. _____

_____

Write at least two additional words that have the suffix *-ent.* Write a definition for each word.

1. _____

_____

2. _____

_____

Create two original sentences using the four additional words you wrote above. Each sentence should contain two of the words.

_____

_____

_____

Name _____ Date _____

Sentence Types

Focus

- A **declarative** sentence makes a statement. It always ends with a period.

- An **interrogative** sentence asks a question. It ends with a question mark.

- An **imperative** sentence gives a command or makes a request. It usually ends with a period.

- An **exclamatory** sentence expresses a strong feeling. It ends with an exclamation point.

- My best friend is Reynaldo.

- Did you see the goal Ana made?

- Please call the police.

- That was a yummy dessert!

Apply On a separate sheet of paper, write a short paragraph about your school day routine or the preparation for a school event. Use each sentence type twice in your paragraph. Trade papers with a partner and identify each sentence type in each other's paragraphs.

Name _____ Date _____

Word Relationships

Focus As you read, you will notice that many words relate to each other because they are about the same topic. These **word relationships** can give you clues about the meanings of unfamiliar words.

Apply Select three relationship topics from the options below. On a separate sheet of paper, write at least five words related to each topic. Try to find one or more words that can be used in all of the groups.

the Lewis and Clark Expedition

a visit to a planetarium

collecting newspapers for recycling

playing in a band

a rodeo

Name _____ Date _____

Selection Vocabulary

Focus

enslaved	bundled	trek	prospering	straddled
rickety	challenge	lasso	association	stunt

Apply Write four sentences on the lines below. Each sentence should use two or more of the selection vocabulary words listed in the Focus box. Make sure each sentence clearly expresses the meaning of the word.

_____

_____

_____

_____

_____

_____

_____

_____

_____

_____

_____

_____

_____

_____

_____

_____

Vocabulary • *Challenge Activities*

Name _____ Date _____

Fact and Opinion

Focus Good writers use both facts and opinions in their writing. A good reader can tell one from the other.

- **Facts** are details that can be proven true or false.

- **Opinions** are what people think. They cannot be proven true or false.

Apply When authors write to persuade, they are very likely to include opinions and try to get their readers to agree with their opinions. One key to good persuasive writing is that the opinions are supported by facts. Choose a topic related to "Going West" about which you have a strong opinion. Then, on a separate sheet of paper, write a paragraph about that topic. Remember that your goal is to persuade readers to agree with your opinion. Be sure to support your opinion with facts.

Spelling

Focus granddaughter   angle

Apply *Granddaughter* **is a compound word. Write three other compound words that begin with the word** *grand* **and define each word.**

_____

_____

_____

Write the definition of *angle* **on the lines below. Write two different definitions for the homograph.**

_____

_____

_____

Use *angle* **in two original sentences. Create one sentence for each meaning you provided above.**

1. _____

_____

2. _____

_____

Spelling • *Challenge Activities*

Name _____ Date _____

Colon and Semicolon

Focus
- **Colons** (:) are used to introduce lists, to separate the minutes and hours of a precise time, and at the end of a business letter's salutation.

- **Semicolons** (;) are used to join independent clauses in a sentence and to help separate clauses joined by some adverbs like *however, therefore,* and *yet*. Use a semicolon when conjunctions like *and* or *but* are <u>not</u> used.

Apply **Write sentences using the following instructions.**

1. Show the correct use of a semicolon in a sentence describing what you did last weekend.

   _____

   _____

2. Make a list of items you always bring to school.

   _____

   _____

3. Write a sentence including what time you got up this morning.

   _____

   _____

4. On a separate sheet of paper, write a business letter. In the body of the letter, use a semicolon at least twice.

5. On a separate sheet of paper, write three compound sentences using no conjunctions.

Name _____ Date _____

Antonyms and Synonyms

Focus

- **Synonyms** are words with the same, or nearly the same, meaning. For example, *giant, huge,* and *massive* are all synonyms.

- **Antonyms** are words that have opposite, or nearly opposite, meanings. An antonym for *empty* is *full,* and an antonym for *dull* is *exciting.*

Apply   **Read the following article about the ghost town of Cerro Gordo. On a separate sheet of paper, write two synonyms and two antonyms for each of the underlined words.**

Cerro Gordo is Spanish for "fat hill." The town is known for being the biggest silver and lead producer in California. Founded in the early 1870s by Mortimer Belshaw and Victor Beaudry, Cerro Gordo produced 100–150 bars of silver every day at its peak. These bars, or loaves, as they were called, weighed a heavy eighty-three pounds each and looked like a loaf of bread.

The silver loaves were shipped by wagon to the port at Los Angeles. At that time, Los Angeles was just a cow town of 2,800 people. According to the edition of the Los Angeles News for February 2, 1872, "Cerro Gordo trade is invaluable. What Los Angeles is, is mainly due to it. It is the silver cord that binds our present existence."

Today, the city of Los Angeles is home to almost 4 million people. It is second in size only to New York City. Los Angeles County is the largest in the United States with a population of close to 10 million people.

Word Structure • *Challenge Activities*

Name _____ Date _____

Selection Vocabulary

Focus

longed	evidence	tattered	trough	territory
centuries	minerals	prosperity	traces	inhabitants

Apply Write four sentences on the lines below. Each
sentence should use two or more of the selection
vocabulary words listed in the Focus box. Make sure each
sentence clearly expresses the meaning of the word.

_____

_____

_____

_____

_____

_____

_____

_____

_____

_____

_____

_____

_____

_____

Name _____ Date _____

Spelling

Focus   specialization   miniature

Apply   Write the definitions of the words *specialization* and *miniature* below. Then use the words together in one original sentence.

specialization _____

_____

miniature _____

_____

Sentence _____

_____

List two words that are synonyms for the word *miniature*.

_____

List two words that would be antonyms for the word *miniature*.

_____

Name _____ Date _____

Transition Words

Copyright © SRA/McGraw-Hill. Permission is granted to reproduce this page for classroom use.

Focus | **Transition words** structure descriptions having to do with time, place, and order. They also signal readers to expect comparisons, contrasts, additional information, and summaries. Some form two or more word phrases.

Apply | **On a separate sheet of paper, rewrite the paragraph, inserting transition words to help this paragraph read more smoothly.**

Doctors warn that people are eating too much salt in their daily diets. These experts have estimated that the consumption of five grams of salt per day is all right for most people. Doctors claim that many people consume between ten and twenty-four grams of salt daily. They advise patients to restrict or even eliminate the use of salt in cooking or at the table. Doctors encourage patients to avoid some processed foods that contain salt as an additive.

Read the list of topics, and write the type of transition words you might use to improve the sentences about the topic.

Paragraph Topic	Transition-Word Type
Winning the Championship	_____
The Beautiful Coast	_____
Making Vegetable Soup	_____
Reducing Sports Injuries	_____

Name _____ Date _____

Language/Word Structure

Focus Understanding **language/word structure** can help you discover the meanings of words. As you read, you will encounter many words that consist of base or root words combined with prefixes, suffixes, or both prefixes and suffixes. Looking at the individual parts of a word's structure can help you determine the word's definition.

Apply Select prefixes, suffixes, and root or base words from the box below to create longer words. On a separate sheet of paper, write each word you form and its definition. On a separate sheet of paper, use each word in a sentence. Consult a dictionary if necessary.

Prefixes				
mis-	*counter-*	*non-*	*un-*	*semi-*
Suffixes				
-able	*-ical*	*-ly*	*-wise*	*-en*
Roots				
sense	take	annual	comfort	clock

Word Structure • *Challenge Activities*

Name _____ Date _____

Selection Vocabulary

Focus

regard	merciful	predict	accurate	drought
prairie	desperately	sowing	heaved	dispositions

Apply Write a free verse poem using at least five of the selection vocabulary words listed in the Focus box.

_____

_____

_____

_____

_____

_____

_____

_____

_____

_____

_____

_____

_____

_____

_____

_____

Name _____ Date _____

Cause and Effect

Focus When one event causes another to happen, the events have a **cause-and-effect relationship.**

- A **cause** is the reason that an event happens.

- An **effect** is the result of a cause.

- Writers use words such as *because, since, therefore,* and *so* to show the reader that a cause-and-effect relationship has taken place.

Apply Practice writing relationships with multiple causes and effects in the space provided below.

One cause with several effects:

_____

_____

_____

_____

One effect with several causes:

_____

_____

_____

_____

Name _____ Date _____

Spelling

Focus Icelandic worrisome

Apply Write the definitions of the words *Icelandic* and *worrisome* below. Then use the words together in one original sentence.

Icelandic _____

_____

worrisome _____

_____

Sentence _____

_____

Identify the base word of *worrisome* and provide at least three additional words that share the base word.

_____

_____

_____

Name _____ Date _____

Appositives and Participial Phrases

Focus

Rule	Example
• An **appositive** is a word or group of words that rename another word in the same sentence.	• My school, **DuBois Elementary,** is a fun place to learn.
• An **appositive phrase** consists of an appositive and the words that modify it.	• Uncle Chris went to France, **a country in Europe,** to study art.
• A **participial phrase** includes a verb and other words in the phrase that modify a noun or pronoun.	• The bike, **leaning quietly against the wall,** reflected sunlight onto the ground.

Apply   Use the appositives and participial phrases in the box below to create a tall tale. On a separate sheet of paper, write two paragraphs using the phrases listed below.

Appositives

the prettiest, spunkiest woman in Tennessee
that old bear killer
good-hearted but nosy

Participial Phrases

putting on like they were just out for a stroll
letting their curiosity get the best of them
sitting on the front porch swing

---

114 UNIT 5 • Lesson 5   Grammar, Usage, and Mechanics • *Challenge Activities*

Name _____ Date _____

Prefix *im-*

Focus The prefix **im-** means "not or in." When *im-,* meaning "not", is added to the beginning of a word, it creates an antonym of that word. For example, the word *perfect* becomes *imperfect.*

Apply The *im-* prefix can mean "not" or "in." Add the *im-* prefix to each of the following words. Then, beside each word write "not" or "in" to show the meaning of the *im-* prefix in that particular word. Then, choose two words with the *im-* prefix meaning "not" and two words with the meaning "in." On a separate sheet of paper, write a sentence for each.

balance _____

mature _____

migrant _____

mortal _____

moveable _____

personal _____

plant _____

port _____

practical _____

precise _____

press _____

print _____

Challenge Activities • Word Structure

Name _____ Date _____

Selection Vocabulary

Focus

equator	horrified	tropics	biologist	species
macaw	donations	designed	grateful	monument

Apply Write four sentences on the lines below. Each sentence should use two or more of the selection vocabulary words listed in the Focus box. Make sure your sentences clearly express the meanings of the words.

_____

_____

_____

_____

_____

_____

_____

_____

_____

_____

_____

_____

Name _____ **Date** _____

Author's Purpose

Copyright © SRA/McGraw-Hill. Permission is granted to reproduce this page for classroom use.

Focus
Writers always have a reason for writing. The **author's purpose** can be to inform, to explain, to entertain, or to persuade. An author can have more than one purpose for writing. The author's purpose affects the details, descriptions, pictures, and dialogue included in a story.

Apply
On a separate sheet of paper, write two paragraphs. Both paragraphs will be about the same topic, but each will have a different purpose. You may choose from the following purposes for your paragraphs: to inform, to explain, to entertain, or to persuade. When you finish, trade papers with a partner, and guess the purpose of his or her paragraphs.

Name _____ Date _____

Spelling

 **Focus**   bureaucrat   biodegradable

 **Apply**   **Write the definitions of the words *bureaucrat* and *biodegradable* below. Then, use the words together in one original sentence.**

bureaucrat _____

_____

_____

biodegradable _____

_____

_____

Sentence _____

_____

_____

Provide two additional words in the same root word family as *bureaucrat:*

_____

Keeping in mind the definition, list some materials that are *biodegradable:*

_____

Name _____ **Date** _____

Helping Verbs and Linking Verbs

Focus

- **Helping verbs,** also known as auxiliary verbs, work with a sentence's main verb to show action or to express a state of being.

Constance **will** attend camp this summer.

The workers **have** finished the building.

- **Linking verbs** are state-of-being verbs that connect the subject to a noun, pronoun, or adjective in the predicate.

That painting **is** beautiful.

They **were** ready for a vacation.

Apply

Helping Verbs			
have	were	been	could
should	might	did	will

Linking Verbs	
appear	seem
taste	became

On a separate sheet of paper, use the helping and linking verbs listed in the box in original sentences. Use each helping verb at least once and each linking verb at least twice. Try to combine different verbs in one sentence. Make sure to use the linking verbs correctly.

Name _____ Date _____

Levels of Specificity

Focus When writers want to effectively describe something, they will try not to use a general word, but a word that is more specific and paints a clearer picture for the reader. Here are two sentences with the same message, yet one uses specific words and one less specific terms:

We were impressed with the entertainer who loudly announced the next act—the animals.

We were impressed with the ringmaster who loudly announced the next act—the lions.

Apply The following series contain words that go from more specific to less specific or from less specific to more specific. Write a word on each line that fits the series.

1. mouth, _____, incisor

2. _____, novel, book

3. North America, _____, Miami

4. bumblebee, _____, animal

5. _____, conifer, tree

6. neighborhood, house, _____

7. peas, _____, food

8. school supply, writing utensil, _____

9. calendar, _____, August

10. body of water, _____, Lake Tahoe

Word Structure • *Challenge Activities*

Name _____ Date _____

Selection Vocabulary

Focus

assassins	challenged	worthy	throb	hideous
strait	destiny	glistening	pity	gaping

Apply The first sentence in a story should grab the reader's attention. If the opening sentence is poorly written or boring, the reader will likely lose interest in reading the rest of the story.

On a separate sheet of paper, using the selection vocabulary words, rewrite the sentences below to make them more interesting.

Example: John Wilkes Booth was responsible for the death of Abraham Lincoln. (assassin)

The assassin, John Wilkes Booth, horrified a nation that night at Ford's theatre, when he murdered Abraham Lincoln.

1. The door was open, so I walked in. (gaping)

2. A cat sat by my window last night crying. (hideous)

3. The woman killed a spider. (pity)

4. "That's my dog," Bob said. (raged)

5. The sun was shining on the snow. (glistening)

6. I watched my paper boat go from one pond to the other. (strait)

7. The noise bothered me. (throb)

8. The sun made my cheeks turn red. (scorched)

Name _____   **Date** _____

Spelling

Focus   aeronautics   geographical

Apply   **Write the definitions of the words *aeronautics* and *geographical* below. Then, use the words together in one original sentence.**

*aeronautics*_____

_____

geographical _____

_____

Sentence_____

_____

Using a dictionary, list five additional words that begin with the same Greek root as *aeronautics*:

_____

Using the letters in the word *geographical*, spell at least six other words and write them on the line.

Example: *hip*

_____

_____

Name _____ Date _____

Compound Sentences

Focus

A **compound sentence** consists of two or more simple sentences, which are also called independent clauses. The sentences should be connected by only a comma and a conjunction, such as *and, or,* or *but,* or by only a semicolon.

Example: I returned the library books late, and I had to pay a fine.

Apply

Using each of the conjunctions in the box, create four compound sentences. One sentence should use a semicolon instead of a conjunction. Write all four sentences on the lines below.

and	or	but

_____

_____

_____

_____

_____

_____

_____

_____

_____

Name _____ Date _____

Irregular Plurals

Focus The plural form of many words is formed by adding -s or -es. **Irregular plurals** do not follow any rule for forming the plural.
Examples: man, men; foot, feet; sheep, sheep; deer, deer

Apply On a separate sheet of paper, write original sentences using the plural form of each word in the box. Be sure each sentence clearly demonstrates the word's meaning. Make sure to use the correct plural form. Trade papers with a partner and identify the plurals in each other's sentences.

cactus	hypothesis	mouse	stimulus
species	man	child	person

Word Structure • *Challenge Activities*

Name _____ **Date** _____

Selection Vocabulary

Focus

sport	descended	quest	beaded	task
lumbered	exhausted	loyalty	spring	fitter

Apply Suppose "The Quest for Healing" was an event that had actually happened in your area or town. On a separate sheet of paper, write a newspaper article describing the events of "The Quest for Healing." Use each selection vocabulary word at least once in your article. Share your article with the class.

Name _____ Date _____

Spelling

Focus thoroughness   companionship

Apply Write the definitions of the words *companionship* and *thoroughness* below. Then, use the words together in one original sentence.

companionship _____

_____

_____

thoroughness _____

_____

_____

Sentence _____

_____

_____

List two words that would be antonyms for the word *companionship*.

_____

_____

List two words that would be antonyms for the word *thoroughness*.

_____

_____

Name _____ Date _____

Prepositional Phrases

Focus

Rule	**Example**
• A **preposition** relates a noun or pronoun to the rest of a sentence.	• He visited the house **near** the river.
• A **prepositional phrase** is a group of words that begins with a preposition and ends with the *object* of the preposition.	• near the *river*

Apply On a separate sheet of paper, write a paragraph comparing and contrasting "The Quest for Healing" and "Jason and the Golden Fleece." You might compare the quests included in both texts, or contrast the reasons for each quest. In your paragraph, use each of the prepositions listed below at least once in a prepositional phrase. Trade papers with a partner and identify the prepositional phrases in each other's paragraphs.

about with	before between	behind since	during to

Name _____ Date _____

Possessives

Copyright © SRA/McGraw-Hill. Permission is granted to reproduce this page for classroom use.

Focus

Possessive nouns are nouns that show ownership or possession of things or qualities.

- Most possessives are formed by adding 's.
- For plural nouns that already end in s, just add an apostrophe.

- Jess's house, a dog's collar
- the cars' horns, zebras' stripes

Apply

1. **Write a sentence using a singular proper possessive noun.**

   _____

   _____

2. **Write a sentence using a plural proper possessive noun.**

   _____

   _____

3. **Write two sentences using both a possessive pronoun and a plural possessive noun.**

   _____

   _____

4. **Write a sentence using two singular possessive nouns.**

   _____

   _____

Name _____ Date _____

Selection Vocabulary

Focus

Paraguay	murals	irritably	pleading	burdened
noble	scowls	intricate	murmur	rare

Apply Create brief clues for each of the selection vocabulary words listed in the Focus box. Do not use any words or phrases in your clues specifically mentioned in the words' definitions located in the glossary. Trade papers with another student in your group, and try to determine the vocabulary word being described.

_____

_____

_____

_____

_____

_____

_____

_____

_____

_____

_____

_____

Name _____ Date _____

Spelling

Focus   preoperational   preadolescence

Apply   Write the definitions of the words *preoperational* and
preadolescence below. Then, use the words together
in one original sentence.

preoperational _____

_____

_____

*preadolescence*_____

_____

_____

Sentence _____

_____

_____

List two words that would be antonyms for the word *preoperational.*

_____

_____

List two words that would be antonyms for the word *preadolescence.*

_____

_____

Name _____ Date _____

Complex Sentences

Focus A **complex sentence** contains an independent clause (simple sentence) and one or more dependent clauses.

Vernon did not start dinner until his sister returned from the store.

Apply **Read the following story. On a separate sheet of paper, convert the underlined sentences into complex sentences.**

Levi Strauss left behind four nephews to follow in his footsteps. The inventor of blue jeans was well respected. He was greatly missed. When the devastating earthquake rocked San Francisco in 1906, Levi's store, factory, and business offices were destroyed in the three-day fire that followed. The company Levi had left behind was solid. His nephews were able to rebuild the factory and store. They continued their Uncle Levi's tradition of sound business practices and generosity by continuing to pay employees. They extended credit to less fortunate merchants.

This inventor of the world-famous American product was born in Bavaria on February 26, 1829. Levi was 18 years old when he immigrated to New York with his mother and sisters. He worked in his brothers' dry goods business until becoming a citizen of the United States six years later. He moved to San Francisco. He imported clothing and fabrics for stores that supplied miners and settlers.

Homophones

Focus | **Homophones** are words that sound the same but have different spellings and meanings. The following word pairs are examples of homophones.

there, their; would, wood; made, maid

Apply | Write a homophone for the underlined word in each sentence. Then, write a sentence using both homophones. Be sure the sentence clearly demonstrates the words' meanings.

The nurse looked over the list of <u>patients</u>.

1. _____

_____

My Aunt Betty always tells me how much I have <u>grown</u>.

2. _____

_____

The Giants <u>won</u> the softball game today.

3. _____

_____

The <u>herd</u> of elephants was running wild through the jungle.

4. _____

_____

Name _____ **Date** _____

Selection Vocabulary

Focus

soiled	lunged	distract	amusing	imitating
sulking	aromas	remark	disturbed	insistently

Apply Write four sentences on the lines below. Each sentence should use two or more of the selection vocabulary words listed in the Focus box. Make sure your sentences clearly express the meanings of the words.

_____

_____

_____

_____

_____

_____

_____

_____

_____

_____

_____

Challenge Activities • Vocabulary

Name _____ Date _____

Making Inferences

Focus Writers often do not include every detail about a character or an event in the story. Readers must use clues from the text to make inferences in order to complete the picture. **Making inferences** means using the writer's clues and your own prior knowledge and experiences to develop a better understanding of the character or event.

Apply The *theme* of a selection is its moral or meaning. The themes of fiction selections often focus on topics that are important to all people in some way. For example, love, friendship, family, and growing up are some popular theme topics. In order to determine a selection's theme, sometimes the reader must make inferences.

Write what you think the theme is for "The Story of Annie Sullivan." Then on a separate sheet of paper, write the clues from the story and the prior knowledge you used to infer the selection's moral or meaning.

Inferred Theme: _____

_____

Comprehension Skill • *Challenge Activities*

Name _____ **Date** _____

Spelling

Focus   spectacular   immobilize

Apply   Write the definitions of the words *spectacular* and *immobilize* below. Then, use the words together in one original sentence.

spectacular _____

_____

immobilize _____

_____

Sentence _____

_____

List two words that would be antonyms for the words *spectacular* and *immobilize.*

_____

_____

List two words that would be synonyms for the words *spectacular* and *immobilize.*

_____

_____

Name _____ Date _____

Misused Modifiers, Pronouns, and Verbs

Focus An important part of writing well is being able to recognize misused words. By carefully revising what you have written and listening closely to how each word has been used, you can spot verbs, pronouns, and modifiers that have been used incorrectly.

Apply Write sentences using the following instructions.

1. Use *lie* in a sentence about the beach.

_____

2. Use *lay* (as in placing) in a sentence about the beach.

_____

3. Use *it's* in a sentence about a mouse.

_____

4. Use *its* in a sentence about a whale.

_____

5. Use *whose* in a sentence about a cat.

_____

6. Use *who's* in a sentence.

_____

Grammar, Usage, and Mechanics • *Challenge Activities*

Challenge Activities Answer Key

p. 68
3.5 Electronic Technology: Revising Text
Cutting and Pasting

The cut and paste icons allow you to move a word, sentence, paragraph, or even a whole document from one place to another. First, highlight the text you want to move. Then click on the cut icon (a pair of scissors). Next, move the cursor to the place you want the text to be. Then click on the paste icon (a clipboard), and your text will be moved to the new location.

p. 81
4.3 Spelling

planet
rhythm

p. 91
4.5 Subject and Verb Agreement

NASA radar was used to locate a lost plane that crashed in the mountains of Montana. This radar detects things through clouds, leaves, brush, and even darkness. When weather, trees, and steep mountains make it difficult to find downed planes, NASA's radar could save lives. Scientists are working on ways to make this technology available for immediate search and rescue missions.

p. 115
6.1 Prefix *im-*

imbalance- not
immature- not
immigrant- in
immortal- not
immoveable- not
impersonal- not
implant- in
import- in
impractical- not
imprecise- not
impress- in
imprint- in

14

22

30

40

44

W9-ANR-245

Better Homes and Gardens®

LOW-. Calorie
RECIPES

Copyright © 2008 Meredith Corporation
All rights reserved. Printed in China.
Excerpted from Better Homes and Gardens®
Best Ever Low-Cal Recipes, 2003.
ISBN: 978-0-696-24087-4

lose weight, feel great!

Are you overweight or overfat? How much can you eat and still lose weight? Can certain foods make you fat? Read on to learn the basics about healthy weight loss.

do you need to lose weight?

One in three American adults is overweight. Are you one of them? Perhaps a better question to ask is, are you overfat? The extra body weight from fat is what increases your risk for developing health problems such as high blood pressure, heart disease, gallstones, diabetes, and some cancers.

How do you know whether you're carrying too much fat? One way is to calculate your Body Mass Index, (BMI). Unlike your bathroom scale, which only tells you your weight, BMI considers the amount of body fat you're carrying.

According to the National Center for Health Statistics, a BMI of 27.3 or more for women and 27.8 or more for men is considered overweight. A severe weight problem is considered as 32.3 or more for women and 32.1 for men.

To figure your BMI, multiply your weight by 700, then divide by your height (in inches). Divide that number by your height again. For example, a 145-pound woman who stands 5'6" tall has a BMI of 23.

145 pounds x 700 = 101,500 ÷ 66 (5'6") ÷ 66 = 23

Once you calculate your BMI, check the chart, *right*, to see if your weight is putting you at risk for health problems.

Lemon Dessert with Raspberries, recipe on page 40

setting a goal weight

If your BMI suggests you need to lose weight, the next step is to set a healthful goal weight.

The best weight for you is as individual as your fingerprints. And, what you want to weigh isn't always what your body wants to weigh.

Body Mass Index (BMI) Risk for Health Problems

BMI	RISK
20 to 25	Very low
26 to 30	Low
31 to 35	Moderate
36 to 40	High

Source: World Health Organization

To make sure your goal weight is healthful and realistic, ask yourself these questions:

- Am I relying on a weight chart to find the best weight for me? Is it realistic? Remember, weight charts are general guidelines. The best weight for you may be higher or lower than the chart indicates.
- Is my goal weight realistic for me? Don't try to look like a tall, skinny fashion model if you are short and big boned. Instead, set a goal that suits your particular build.
- Can I comfortably maintain my goal weight without constant dieting and exercising? A healthful weight is one you can maintain by eating moderate portions of a wide variety of foods, and by getting moderate amounts of regular physical activity.

figure your calorie needs

How many calories do you need each day to reach your goal weight? It depends on several factors including your age, body size, and activity level.

A pound of body fat contains approximately 3,500 calories (about the same number as in a pound of butter or margarine). If you eat 3,500 fewer calories than your body uses, you will shed about one pound.

Use the steps below to estimate the calories you need each day to lose about 1 pound per week.

1. Multiply your current weight in pounds by the amount of calories you burn each day based on your average level of activity:
- 13 calories/pound for inactivity (sitting most of the day, such as doing office work)
- 15 calories/pound for moderate activity (office work plus 30 to 60

> ### Sample Calorie Calculation
>
> If you're:
>
> **133 pounds, moderately active**
>
> **133 x 15 = 1,995 calories per day to maintain your weight**
>
> **1,995 – 500 calories per day = 1,495 calories per day to lose about 1 pound per week**
>
> *Source:* World Health Organization

minutes of aerobic activity, or walking/standing most of the day)
- 17 calories/pound for extensive activity (strenuous physical work or an athletic level of physical activity)

2. Subtract 500 calories from your daily calorie needs in Step 1 to determine the number of calories you need to lose about 1 pound per week.

Create a daily deficit of 500 calories per day by eating fewer calories, burning off extra calories with physical activity, or, best yet, doing a combination of both.

You can do this in different ways. For example, each day you could eat 400 fewer calories and burn off 100 extra calories with physical activity, or eat 300 fewer calories and burn off 200 extra calories. Whatever the combination, the choice is yours.

Don't cut calories severely! It's difficult to get all the nutrients you need when you eat fewer than 1,200 calories per day. Most dietitians and health experts don't recommend going below this calorie level without the supervision of a doctor.

all calories count—but not all calories are equal

Food is a combination of carbohydrates, protein, and/or fat. These nutrients provide the calories found in all foods. But not all calories are created equal. Carbohydrates and protein yield four calories per gram, while fat yields nine calories per gram. Alcohol also contributes calories—about seven calories per gram—but has little nutritional value.

When you compare an equal amount of fat to an equal amount of carbohydrate or protein, fat packs more than twice the calories per gram of either. That's why fatty foods are generally high in calories. But all calories count. Eating more calories than your body needs—whether from carbohydrates, protein, or fat—results in weight gain.

nutrition by the numbers

Eat less than 30 percent of your calories from fat. Eat more fiber. Don't eat too much sodium. Sound nutrition advice. But how do you apply this advice to the food choices you make each day?

Check out the daily guidelines chart, *below*, for healthful amounts to consume for several key nutrients,

based on daily calorie levels of 1,200, 1,500, 2,000, and 2,500. The guidelines for 2,000 calories are the basis for the Daily Values on the Nutrition Facts food label, so reading labels is an essential tool for creating a healthful meal plan.

Remember, these are guidelines, not exact targets you must hit each day. Balancing your food choices over time is the key to maintaining your weight. (*See sample menus, page 10.*)

get active: you've got everything to gain

To win at weight loss, burning calories through activity is just as important as adopting a healthful eating plan. No matter how you look at it, physical activity comes up a winner. Regular physical activity:

- Burns calories and preserves lean muscle mass
- Helps maintain your weight once you reach your goal
- Revs up your metabolism so you continue to burn extra calories for up to several hours
- Strengthens bones and muscles
- Reduces risk of heart disease, high blood pressure, diabetes
- Makes you feel good by reducing feelings of depression and anxiety

Daily Guidelines CALORIES *	1,200	1,500	2,000	2,500
Total Fat	40 g	50 g	65 g	80 g
Saturated Fat	12 g	15 g	20 g	25 g
Cholesterol	300 mg	300 mg	300 mg	300 mg
Sodium	2,400 mg	2,400 mg	2,400 mg	2,400 mg
Total Carbohydrate	180 g	225 g	300 g	375 g
Dietary Fiber	20 g	20 g	25 g	30 g

* If your calorie intake differs, adjust these guidelines accordingly.

activities to boost your losses

This chart shows several options for fitting physical activity into your day. Each activity burns about 150 calories in the time indicated.

√ Washing and waxing a car for 45 to 60 minutes

√ Washing windows or floors for 45 to 60 minutes

  Playing basketball for 15 to 20 minutes

  Playing volleyball for 45 minutes

√ Gardening for 30 to 45 minutes

√ Walking 1¾ miles in 35 minutes (20 min./mile)

  Basketball (shooting baskets) for 30 minutes

  Bicycling 5 miles in 30 minutes

  Dancing fast for 30 minutes

  Pushing a stroller 1½ miles in 30 minutes

√ Raking leaves for 30 minutes

√ Walking 2 miles in 30 minutes (15 min./mile)

  Water aerobics for 30 minutes

  Swimming laps for 20 minutes

  Bicycling 4 miles in 15 minutes

  Jumping rope for 15 minutes

  Running 1½ miles in 15 minutes (10 min./mile)

  Shoveling snow for 15 minutes

√ Stair climbing for 15 minutes

less vigorous, more time

more vigorous, less time

Source: U.S. Department of Health and Human Services (A Report of the Surgeon General, 1996)

Note: If you have health problems or are a man over the age of 40 or a woman over the age of 50, consult your doctor before you begin a new physically active program.

Breakfast Blintzes, recipe on page 19

To reap these benefits, health experts recommend striving for a moderate amount of physical activity on a daily basis. The chart on *page 5* shows several options for fitting moderate physical activity into your day. Each activity burns about 150 calories in the time indicated. For best results, choose a variety of activities you enjoy and that fit easily into your lifestyle.

keeping weight off—you've got what it takes

Once you've reached your goal weight, you'll likely worry about keeping those pounds off.

Relax. You've already got what it takes. It's simply a matter of continuing the same healthful eating and activity habits that helped you meet your goal—habits that become part of your daily living.

More good news: You can enjoy more calories each day to maintain your weight. Use step 1 from the Figure Your Calorie Needs section on page 3 to calculate the number of calories you need for weight maintenance. Spend these extra

calories wisely by choosing a variety of nutrient-dense foods. Of course an occasional treat is fine, too.

If your weight creeps up a pound or two—say over the holidays or during a vacation—don't worry. Even people who are naturally thin experience weight fluctuations at certain times. Just resume your healthful habits as soon as possible, and the pounds will come off again. Remember: Maintaining your weight is all about choices. You can still enjoy favorite foods as long as you watch your portions and stay active.

healthy living is good for the entire family

Eat right and get fit. This isn't just advice for people trying to lose weight. It's important for people of all ages. Make delicious low-fat recipes part of your regular dinner rotation. Introduce your kids to lower-fat snacks and lunches. Make time for activities that keep the whole family moving—walking, basketball, swimming. When the entire family is involved, you'll find it easier to maintain your new healthful lifestyle.

Hearty Italian-Style Soup, recipe on page 27

diet myths

Have you heard the one about the fat-burning grapefruit? Or the Chinese magic weight-loss earrings? Have you tried a get-thin-quick scheme or two yourself? You're not alone!

Diet gimmicks waste your money because they don't work. Here are the facts about five popular weight-loss fads.

Fad: Fasting is a quick, effective way to take off pounds.

Fact: Quite the contrary. Fasting for long periods is dangerous and counterproductive. Any quick weight loss you see is mostly from water and muscle tissue, not body fat. Going without food for long periods deprives you of energy and nutrients. It also slows down your metabolism so you burn fewer calories—not a desirable consequence!

Fad: Try the Cabbage Soup Diet. The more soup you eat, the more weight you'll lose.

Fact: On this seven-day diet you fill up on all the cabbage soup you want, while other foods are strictly limited. There's no magic about cabbage soup. If you lose weight, it's only because you're eating fewer calories. This diet is nutritionally unbalanced and doesn't teach healthful, new habits. You'll most likely gain back any weight you lose.

Fad: A high-protein, low-carbohydrate diet triggers quick weight loss by causing the body to burn stored fat.

Fact: Rapid weight loss on this diet is mostly from water, not body fat, so you'll likely regain the weight. Depriving the body of fuel from carbohydrates can cause nausea, weakness, breakdown of muscle, dehydration, and stress on the kidneys, all of which are potentially dangerous. Because this diet forbids almost all fruits, vegetables, breads, cereals, and other grains, you'll come up short on vitamins, minerals, and fiber.

Fad: Chromium supplements stimulate your body to use stored fat so you can eat whatever you want and still lose weight.

Fact: Pills—including chromium supplements—can't stimulate your body to burn fat. Most people get all the chromium they need from food. Taking extra chromium in pill form doesn't appear to offer any benefits, and may cause harm.

Fad: Diet pills are an easy way to take off excess pounds.

Fact: Over-the-counter diet pills curb your appetite, but only work for a few weeks. Some pills may cause dangerous side effects. And be careful with herbal diet aids. Just because a pill is made with herbs does not make it safe. Always consult your doctor about over-the-counter or prescription diet aids.

low-fat flavor boosters

To cook low-fat, yet full-flavored, dishes, stock your pantry and refrigerator with some of these fabulous flavor boosters. The next time your food needs perking up, you'll be ready for action. Experiment by adding a small amount of the ingredient first, then season to taste.

- Lemon, lime, and orange juices. Great for fish and beef dishes, pasta, and salad dressings.
- Light soy sauce and teriyaki sauce. Add to marinades for meat and poultry, savory sauces, and vegetable dishes.
- Red and green onions, leeks, and shallots. Sauté and add to main dishes and soups or slice raw and add to pizza and salads.
- Salsas. Spice up soups, gravies, and sauces with a spoonful; spread on a pizza shell instead of pizza sauce; toss with pasta.
- Chutneys (such as mango, peach, and pear). Serve alongside grilled and broiled meats, with rice dishes, or as a spread in grilled meat and cheese sandwiches.
- Asian ingredients (such as cilantro, chili paste, and hoisin sauce). Experiment by adding to broth soups, pasta, salads, and stir-fry dishes.
- Fresh and dried herbs. Add to salad dressings, marinades, and soups. Sprinkle on top of pizzas, entrées (as a garnish), and salads. As a rule of thumb, use two or three times as much snipped fresh herb as dry herb.

- Dried herb mixtures. Save money and time and experience unique flavor combinations with herb mixtures such as Cajun seasoning, lemon-dill, Beau Monde seasoning, five-spice powder, Italian blend, and Jamaican jerk seasoning.
- Bottled hot pepper sauces. Shake a few drops into dishes that could use a little heat.
- Flavored pepper seasonings. Great for grilling, these seasonings include lemon pepper, garlic pepper, and herb pepper.
- Flavored vinegars. Look for herbed, balsamic, champagne, fruit, and wine vinegars. Flavored vinegars add a real boost to salad dressings and most other recipes that call for vinegar.
- Roasted garlic. To roast a head of garlic, cut off the pointed top and place cut side up in a baking dish. Drizzle with a little olive oil and bake, covered, in a 400° oven about 25 minutes or until soft. Use the cloves as a bread spread or add to main dishes, sauces, or mashed potatoes. The flavor will be mild and smooth.

No-Fry French Toast,
recipe on page 20

Sugar and Spice Popcorn,
recipe on page 46

- **Fresh grated ginger.** Peel and grate this root, then add to both sweet and savory foods, starting with ½ teaspoon or so and adding more to taste.
- **Fresh grated citrus peel (such as lemon, lime, and orange).** Add to vegetables, baked goods, salad dressings, rice, couscous, and pasta dishes.
- **Mustard.** Choose from the many varieties of mustards, including honey, spicy, coarse-grain brown, herb, peppercorn, sweet-hot, and Chinese.
- **Roasted red peppers.** These come bottled for convenience and add a smoky, sweet pepper taste. Try them in appetizer spreads, main dishes, and salads.
- **Full-flavored oils.** Just a quick drizzle of chili, sesame, hazelnut, walnut, or virgin olive oil offers plenty of rich flavor.
- **Pungent cheeses.** Aged Parmesan, blue cheese, sharp cheddar, goat cheese, and feta cheese have bold enough flavors that a little goes a long way. Sprinkle small amounts on top of main dish salads for a more satisfying and flavorful meal.

Biscotti,
recipe on page 47

Chicken and Penne with Basil Sauce,
recipe on page 33

7-day menu plan

	Breakfast	Lunch
DAY 1	1½ cups cornflakes ½ cup fat-free milk ½ cup orange juice	Potato Soup (page 23) 1 bran raisin muffin 1 teaspoon margarine
For 1,500 calories add:	½ English muffin, toasted ½ teaspoon margarine	1 small apple
DAY 2	Granola (page 17) ½ cup grapefruit juice	Fruited Cottage Cheese Salad (page 28) 2 carrots, cut into sticks 6 whole wheat crackers
For 1,500 calories add:	½ cup grapefruit juice	½ roast beef sandwich (1 slice whole wheat bread, 2 ounces lean roast beef, lettuce, mustard)
DAY 3	1½ cups toasted oat cereal 1 cup fat-free milk ½ pink grapefruit with 1½ teaspoons brown sugar	Tortellini-Vegetable Salad (page 29) ½ cup watermelon cubes 1 cup fat-free milk
For 1,500 calories add:	8 ounces fat-free yogurt, any flavor	1 cup watermelon cubes 5 whole wheat crackers

* Snacks may be eaten any time during the day.

See page 3 to determine your calorie requirements, then use these menus as a guide for a 1,200-calorie-a-day plan (page references tell where to find the recipes). For 1,500 calories, add the foods listed in color. If you need more than 1,500 calories, add foods such as fruit, vegetables, or low-fat dairy products until you're at a calorie level that meets your needs.

Dinner	Snack*
Pork Roast with Pineapple Chutney (page 37) 1 cup cooked corn 2 cups tossed salad 2 tablespoons fat-free Italian salad dressing 1 cup fat-free milk Bread Pudding (page 43)	Tropical Banana Milk Shake (page 48)
$^1/_2$ cup cooked corn 1 ounce shredded reduced-fat cheddar cheese to salad	
Citrus-Tarragon Salmon Steak (page 39) 1 cup steamed broccoli 1 small whole wheat roll 1 teaspoon margarine	Mocha Milk Shake (page 48) 1 small banana
	2 graham crackers (2-$^1/_2$" squares)
Bow Ties and Cheese (page 38) 2 cups tossed salad 2 tablespoons reduced-fat salad dressing 1$^1/_2$ cups fat-free milk $^1/_2$ cup low-fat frozen yogurt	Sugar and Spice Popcorn (page 46)
1 cup cantaloupe chunks	

Note: Unsweetened coffee, tea, and water are suggested beverages. Ideally, you should drink 6 to 8 glasses of water throughout the day.

	Breakfast	Lunch
DAY 4	1 English muffin, toasted 2 teaspoons margarine 8 ounces fat-free yogurt, any flavor	Hearty Italian-Style Soup (page 27) 10 saltine crackers 1 medium orange
For 1,500 calories add:		
DAY 5	Fruity Oatmeal (page 16) 1 cup cubed melon 1 cup fat-free milk	Easy Corn and Bean Salad (page 25) 5 whole-grain crackers 1 cup fat-free milk
For 1,500 calories add:	8 ounces fat-free yogurt, any flavor	
DAY 6	1 cup cooked oatmeal mixed with 1 tablespoon dried cranberries 1/2 cup fat-free milk	1/2 ham sandwich (1 slice whole wheat bread, 1 ounce sliced ham, lettuce, tomato, mustard) Corn Chowder (page 24) 10 baby carrots 1 cup fat-free milk
For 1,500 calories add:	1 bran muffin	1/2 ham sandwich (same as above) 1 medium orange
DAY 7	Brunch Ham and Cheese Frittata (page 15) 1 1/2 cups honeydew and cantaloupe cubes tossed with 1/2 cup fat-free vanilla yogurt 2 slices whole wheat toast 1 cup fat-free milk	
For 1,500 calories add:		

*Snacks may be eaten any time during the day.

Dinner	Snack*
Beef with Mushroom-Tomato Sauce (page 34) ⅔ cup long grain and wild rice pilaf 1 cup steamed asparagus Lemon Dessert with Raspberries (page 41)	2 Biscotti (page 47)
⅓ cup long grain and wild rice pilaf ½ cup steamed, mixed vegetables	1 medium apple 1 tablespoon peanut butter 1 cup fat-free milk
Baked Chimichangas (page 35) 2 cups tossed salad 2 tablespoons fat-free salad dressing Frozen Cranberry Pie (page 43)	3 cups light microwave popcorn
1 ounce shredded mozzarella cheese to salad ½ cup cooked corn	1 medium nectarine
Chicken Cacciatore (page 31) ½ cup hot cooked spaghetti 2 cups tossed salad 2 tablespoons reduced-fat salad dressing 1 small sourdough roll 1 teaspoon margarine 1 cup fresh melon cubes	1 fat-free frozen chocolate sorbet bar
Barbecue-Sauced Beef Sandwich (page 32) 1 cup green and red sweet pepper strips Chocolate-Cinnamon Angel Cake (page 42) ½ cup strawberries	8 ounces fat-free yogurt, any flavor 1 cup fresh blueberries 2 vanilla wafers
	1 ounce pretzels 1 ounce reduced-fat cheddar cheese 1 medium orange

Note: Unsweetened coffee, tea, and water are suggested beverages. Ideally, you should drink 6 to 8 glasses of water throughout the day.

breakfasts

success tips

Before beginning your weight-loss venture, ask yourself why you want to lose weight. Is it because your class reunion looms on the horizon? Is your spouse pushing you to drop some pounds? The best reason to lose weight is for your health, such as wanting to feel more energetic so you can live life to the fullest.

Ham and Cheese Frittata (recipe on page 15)

ham and cheese frittata

Preparation time: *25 minutes*   Broiling time: *2 minutes*

A frittata is an Italian egg dish that resembles an omelet. It is cooked on top of the stove until almost set, then placed under the broiler to finish cooking. A cast-iron skillet works well for both cooking phases *(pictured on page 14)*.

Nonstick cooking spray
1 cup chopped cooked ham (about 5 ounces)
1/2 cup chopped onion
1/2 cup chopped green or red sweet pepper

6 slightly beaten eggs
3/4 cup low-fat cottage cheese
1/8 teaspoon ground black pepper
2 plum tomatoes, thinly sliced
1/4 cup shredded reduced-fat cheddar cheese (1 ounce)

method

1 Coat an unheated 10-inch broiler-proof skillet with nonstick cooking spray. Preheat skillet over medium heat. Add ham, onion, and sweet pepper. Cook about 4 minutes or until vegetables are tender and ham is lightly browned.
2 Meanwhile, in a medium mixing bowl combine eggs, cottage cheese, and black pepper. Pour over ham mixture in skillet.
3 Cook over medium-low heat. As egg mixture sets, run a spatula around the edge of the skillet, lifting the egg mixture so uncooked portion flows underneath. Continue cooking and lifting edge until egg mixture is almost set (surface will be moist).

4 Place skillet under broiler 5 inches from heat. Broil for 1 to 2 minutes or until top is just set.
5 Arrange tomato slices on top of frittata. Sprinkle cheddar cheese over tomato. Broil 1 minute more. Makes 6 servings.

Nutrition facts per serving:
161 calories, 8 g total fat (3 g saturated fat), 231 mg cholesterol, 494 mg sodium, 5 g carbohydrate, 1 g fiber, 17 g protein
Exchanges: 2 Medium-Fat Meat, 1 Vegetable

fruity oatmeal

Start to finish: *15 minutes*

In just 15 minutes you'll have a warm breakfast for a cold winter morning.
If you have a penchant for pears or apricots, substitute them
for the peaches or apple.

2 cups water

1/4 teaspoon salt

1 cup regular rolled oats

1 cup coarsely chopped peeled
peaches or chopped apple

1/4 cup raisins or snipped pitted
whole dates

1/8 teaspoon ground cinnamon

2 teaspoons brown sugar

1/2 cup fat-free milk

method

1 In a medium saucepan bring the
water and salt to boiling; stir in
oats, peaches or apple, raisins or
dates, and cinnamon. Reduce heat.
Simmer, uncovered, for 5 minutes,
stirring occasionally. Remove from
heat. Cover; let stand for 2 minutes.
Stir in brown sugar.

2 Divide the hot oat mixture among
4 bowls. Pour 2 tablespoons of the
milk over each serving. Serve
immediately. Makes 4 servings.

Nutrition facts per serving:

141 calories, 1 g total fat (0 g saturated fat), 1 mg cholesterol, 155 mg
sodium, 29 g carbohydrate,
1 g fiber, 5 g protein

Exchanges: 2 Starch

granola

Preparation time: *15 minutes*   Baking time: *45 minutes*
Cooling time: *30 minutes*

Shredded apples add flavor and texture to this honey-sweetened granola.
Sprinkle the granola over low-fat yogurt for a quick snack
or breakfast on the go.

3 cups regular rolled oats
1 cup coarsely shredded
    unpeeled apple
1/2 cup toasted wheat germ
1/4 cup honey
1/4 cup water

1 1/2 teaspoons ground cinnamon
1 teaspoon vanilla or
    1/2 teaspoon almond extract
Nonstick cooking spray
Fat-free milk

method

1 In a large bowl combine oats,
apple, and wheat germ; mix well. In
a small saucepan stir together
honey, water, and cinnamon. Heat
to boiling; remove from heat. Stir in
vanilla or almond extract. Pour over
oat mixture; mix well.

2 Coat a 15x10x1-inch baking pan
with cooking spray. Spread oat
mixture evenly in pan. Bake in a
325° oven about 45 minutes or
until golden brown, stirring
occasionally. Spread onto foil until
granola is cool. (To store, place

cooled granola in an airtight
container in the refrigerator for up
to 2 weeks.) Serve with milk.
Makes 8 (1/2-cup) servings.

Nutrition facts per serving with 1/3 cup
fat-free milk: 216 calories, 3 g total
fat (1 g saturated fat), 1 mg
cholesterol, 44 mg sodium, 39 g
carbohydrate, 0 g fiber, 10 g protein
Exchanges: 2 Starch, 1/2 Milk

breakfast blintzes

Preparation time: *30 minutes* Baking time: *15 minutes*

Plan a brunch around these ricotta-filled crepes. You can make the crepes up to two days in advance. Layer the cooled crepes between waxed paper and store in an airtight container in the refrigerator.

 1 egg
1$\frac{1}{2}$ cups fat-free milk
 1 cup all-purpose flour
   Nonstick cooking spray
$\frac{1}{2}$ teaspoon shortening
 1 15-ounce carton light ricotta
   cheese

 7 tablespoons orange marmalade
 1 tablespoon sugar
$\frac{1}{8}$ teaspoon ground cinnamon
$\frac{2}{3}$ cup light dairy sour cream
$\frac{1}{2}$ cup fresh raspberries
   or blueberries

method

1 For crepes, combine egg, milk, and flour. Beat with rotary beater until well mixed. Coat an unheated 6-inch skillet or crepe pan with cooking spray. Preheat skillet over medium heat. Remove from heat and pour in about 2 tablespoons batter. Lift and tilt skillet to spread batter. Return skillet to heat; cook 30 to 60 seconds or until browned on 1 side only. Remove from skillet. Repeat with remaining batter to make 15 crepes. Lightly brush skillet with shortening between crepes, as needed.

2 For filling, in a medium mixing bowl combine ricotta cheese, 2 tablespoons of the orange marmalade, the sugar, and cinnamon. Spoon about 2 tablespoons of the filling onto the unbrowned side of

a crepe; spread out slightly. Fold in half. Fold in half again, forming a wedge. Repeat with remaining filling and remaining crepes.

3 Coat a shallow baking pan with nonstick cooking spray. Arrange blintzes in pan. Bake in a 350° oven for 15 to 20 minutes or until heated through. To serve, spoon about 2 teaspoons of the sour cream and 1 teaspoon of the remaining orange marmalade onto each blintz. Sprinkle with berries. Makes 15 blintzes.

Nutrition facts per blintz:
111 calories, 2 g total fat (1 g saturated fat), 21 mg cholesterol, 51 mg sodium, 17 g carbohydrate, 1 g fiber, 6 g protein
Exchanges: 1 Starch, $\frac{1}{2}$ Lean Meat

no-fry french toast

Start to finish: *25 minutes*

Once you try this oven-baked French toast, you'll never make it the old way again. On a griddle or in a skillet, French toast must be made in batches. Baking allows you to make eight pieces at one time.

Nonstick cooking spray
1 slightly beaten egg
1 slightly beaten egg white
3/4 cup fat-free milk
1 teaspoon vanilla
1/8 teaspoon ground cinnamon
8 1/2-inch-thick slices
   French bread

1/4 teaspoon finely shredded
   orange peel
1/2 cup orange juice
1 tablespoon honey
1 teaspoon cornstarch
1/8 teaspoon ground cinnamon
1 tablespoon powdered sugar
   (optional)

method

1 Coat a large baking sheet with cooking spray. In a pie plate combine egg, egg white, milk, vanilla, and 1/8 teaspoon ground cinnamon. Soak bread slices in egg mixture about 1 minute per side. Place on prepared baking sheet.

2 Bake in a 450° oven about 6 minutes or until bread is lightly browned. Turn bread over and bake 5 to 8 minutes more or until golden brown.

3 Meanwhile, for orange syrup, in a small saucepan stir together orange peel, orange juice, honey, cornstarch, and 1/8 teaspoon cinnamon. Cook and stir until thickened and bubbly. Cook and stir 2 minutes more.

4 If desired, sift powdered sugar over toast. Serve with warm orange syrup. Makes 4 servings.

Nutrition facts per serving:
171 calories, 3 g total fat (1 g saturated fat), 54 mg cholesterol, 263 mg sodium, 29 g carbohydrate, 0 g fiber, 7 g protein
Exchanges: 2 Starch

lunches

success tips

Make only a change or two at a time to your eating and activity habits, rather than attempting a complete lifestyle overhaul. You're more likely to stick with new habits when you take the slow approach.

Potato Soup (recipe on page 23)

potato soup

Preparation time: *35 minutes* Cooking time: *20 minutes*

This soup is pureed, so use whatever type of potato you happen
to have on hand. Strain the soup, if you like, to remove
any remaining strands of the celery *(pictured on page 22).*

3 medium potatoes (1 pound),
  peeled and quartered
2 cups water
1/2 cup chopped onion
1/2 cup sliced celery
1/2 cup sliced carrot
1 clove garlic, minced
1 tablespoon snipped
  fresh thyme or 1/2 teaspoon
  dried thyme, crushed

1 teaspoon instant chicken
  bouillon granules
1/8 teaspoon pepper
2 cups fat-free milk
  Snipped fresh chives (optional)
  Edible flowers (optional)

method

1 In a large saucepan combine
potatoes, water, onion, celery,
carrot, garlic, thyme, bouillon
granules, and pepper. Bring to
boiling; reduce heat. Simmer,
covered, for 20 to 25 minutes or
until potatoes are tender. Remove
from heat. Cool slightly. Place, a
portion at a time, in blender
container or food processor bowl.
Cover and process until nearly
smooth. If desired, strain. Return all
to saucepan. Stir in milk; heat just
to boiling. (If desired, divide hot
soup among 4 airtight containers.
Store for up to 3 days in
refrigerator.) If desired, sprinkle
each serving with snipped chives
and garnish with an edible flower.
Makes 4 side-dish servings.

To tote for lunch: Transfer soup to a
preheated insulated vacuum bottle.
(To preheat the vacuum bottle, fill
it with hot tap water. Cover with
the lid and let stand about 5
minutes. Pour out the water and
immediately fill with the hot soup.)
If using chilled soup, transfer to a
small saucepan. Heat just to boiling,
stirring often. Transfer soup to
preheated bottle.

Nutrition facts per serving:
159 calories, 0 g total fat, 2 mg
cholesterol, 314 mg sodium, 33 g
carbohydrate, 3 g fiber, 7 g protein
Exchanges: 1 Starch, 1 Vegetable,
1/2 Milk

corn chowder

Start to finish: *25 minutes*

Chowders are generally cream-based. This lightened version is based on evaporated fat-free milk, which is much lower in calories than cream. Evaporated milk also adds more flavor than regular milk.

1 14¹/₂-ounce can reduced-sodium chicken broth

1 10-ounce package frozen whole kernel corn

1 cup chopped onion

¹/₂ cup chopped red and/or green sweet pepper

¹/₈ teaspoon ground black pepper

1 12-ounce can evaporated fat-free milk

¹/₄ cup all-purpose flour

1 tablespoon snipped fresh parsley (optional)

method

1 In a medium saucepan combine the broth, corn, onion, sweet pepper, and black pepper. Bring to boiling; reduce heat. Simmer, covered, about 5 minutes or until onion is tender.

2 In a small bowl stir together the evaporated milk and flour. Stir into broth mixture. Cook and stir until thickened and bubbly. Cook and stir for 1 minute more. If desired, sprinkle with fresh parsley. Makes 6 side-dish servings.

Nutrition facts per serving:
122 calories, 1 g total fat (0 g saturated fat), 2 mg cholesterol, 261 mg sodium, 23 g carbohydrate, 1 g fiber, 7 g protein
Exchanges: 1 Starch, ½ Milk

_chicken corn chowder 255 calories

Prepare Corn Chowder as directed except, at the end of cooking, stir in 1 cup chopped cooked chicken. Heat through. Makes 3 main-dish servings.

Nutrition facts per serving:
255 calories, 4 g total fat (1 g saturated fat), 36 mg cholesterol, 424 mg sodium, 35 g carbohydrate, 1 g fiber, 22 g protein
Exchanges: 1½ Starch, 2 Lean Meat, ½ Milk

easy corn and bean salad

Preparation time: *20 minutes*   Chilling time: *2 to 8 hours*

Serve this refreshing salad wrapped inside lettuce-lined flour tortillas for a tasty out-of-hand lunch.

1 16-ounce package frozen whole kernel corn

1 15-ounce can dark red kidney beans, rinsed and drained

1/2 cup chopped green sweet pepper

1/2 cup purchased salsa

2 tablespoons snipped fresh cilantro

1/4 teaspoon ground cumin

1 clove garlic, minced
  Lettuce and/or purple kale leaves

method

1 Cook frozen corn according to package directions, except omit any salt and margarine or butter. Drain. Rinse with cold water. Drain.

2 In a large mixing bowl stir together corn, kidney beans, sweet pepper, salsa, cilantro, cumin, and garlic. Cover and refrigerate for at least 2 hours or up to 8 hours.

3 To serve, mound corn mixture on 4 lettuce-lined plates. Makes 4 main-dish servings.

Nutrition facts per serving:
  207 calories, 2 g total fat (0 g saturated fat), 0 mg cholesterol, 293 mg sodium, 46 g carbohydrate, 6 g fiber, 12 g protein
Exchanges: 3 Starch

hearty italian-style soup

Preparation time: *30 minutes*   Cooking time: *20 minutes*

Package this soup in single-serving freezer containers and stockpile a supply in your freezer. You'll be ready for anything—a quick meal, on-the-go lunches, or those days when everyone eats in shifts.

2 $14^{1}/_{2}$-ounce cans beef broth
2 cups shredded cabbage
1 $14^{1}/_{2}$-ounce can low-sodium
   tomatoes, undrained
   and cut up
2 medium potatoes
   (unpeeled, if desired), cubed
$^{1}/_{2}$ cup chopped carrot
$^{1}/_{2}$ cup sliced celery
$^{1}/_{2}$ cup chopped onion
$^{1}/_{4}$ cup snipped fresh parsley

1 teaspoon dried
   Italian seasoning, crushed
$^{1}/_{4}$ teaspoon garlic salt
$^{1}/_{4}$ teaspoon pepper
1 15- or 19-ounce can
   white kidney beans
   (cannellini beans),
   rinsed and drained
$1^{1}/_{2}$ cups chopped cooked beef or
   chicken (about 8 ounces)

method

1 In a large saucepan or Dutch oven combine beef broth, cabbage, undrained tomatoes, potatoes, carrot, celery, onion, parsley, Italian seasoning, garlic salt, and pepper. Bring to boiling; reduce heat. Simmer, covered, about 20 minutes or until vegetables are tender.

2 Stir in the beans and beef or chicken. Cook and stir for 2 to 3 minutes or until heated through. (If desired, divide hot soup among 6 airtight containers. Store up to 3 days in the refrigerator.) Makes 6 main-dish servings.

To tote for lunch: Transfer hot soup to a preheated insulated vacuum bottle. (To preheat the bottle, fill with hot tap water. Cover with lid; let stand about 5 minutes. Pour out water and immediately fill with the hot soup.) If using chilled soup, transfer to a small saucepan. Heat just to boiling, stirring often. Reduce heat. Simmer, covered, for 3 minutes. Transfer soup to preheated bottle.

Nutrition facts per serving:
203 calories, 4 g total fat (1 g saturated fat), 34 mg cholesterol, 711 mg sodium, 28 g carbohydrate, 6 g fiber, 19 g protein

Exchanges: $1^{1}/_{2}$ Starch, 2 Lean Meat, 1 Vegetable

fruited cottage cheese salad

Start to finish: *15 minutes*

Apples, dried fruit, and a dash of cinnamon transform cottage cheese into a satisfying single-serving lunch. To make enough for the whole family, simply double, triple, or quadruple the recipe as needed.

1/2 cup low-fat cottage cheese
 1 small apple, chopped (1/2 cup)
 2 tablespoons mixed dried fruit bits or raisins

Dash ground cinnamon, ground nutmeg, or apple pie spice
 1 lettuce leaf

method

1 In a small mixing bowl stir together cottage cheese; apple; dried fruit bits or raisins; and cinnamon, nutmeg, or apple pie spice. (If desired, cover and refrigerate for up to 24 hours.)
2 To serve, line a plate with lettuce leaf. Spoon cottage cheese mixture on top. Makes 1 main-dish serving.
To tote for lunch: Pack 1 lettuce leaf in a small plastic bag. Place 1 serving of the salad in an airtight container. Place the bag of lettuce and the container of the salad in an insulated lunch box with a frozen ice pack.

Nutrition facts per serving:
163 calories, 2 g total fat (1 g saturated fat), 5 mg cholesterol, 380 mg sodium, 23 g carbohydrate, 1 g fiber, 15 g protein
Exchanges: 2 Lean Meat, 1 Fruit

garden-style cottage cheese 75 calories

1/2 cup fat-free cottage cheese, drained
1/3 cup finely chopped red, green, or yellow sweet pepper
1/3 cup finely shredded carrot
1/4 cup finely chopped green onion
1 1/2 teaspoons Dijon-style mustard

1 In a medium bowl combine cottage cheese, sweet pepper, carrot, green onion, and mustard. Serve immediately or cover and refrigerate for up to 24 hours. Makes 2 main-dish servings.

Nutrition facts per serving:
75 calories, 0 g total fat, 7 mg cholesterol, 208 mg sodium, 7 g carbohydrate, 1 g fiber, 11 g protein
Exchanges: 1 Lean Meat, 1 Vegetable

tortellini-vegetable salad

Preparation time: *20 minutes* Chilling time: *4 to 24 hours*

Simple ingredients turn cheese-filled tortellini into a main-dish salad that's a great make-ahead dish for weekday lunches. Try another variety of frozen vegetables—such as an Italian combination—to suit your taste.

1 9-ounce package refrigerated cheese-filled tortellini

1 10-ounce package frozen peas and carrots

1/2 cup fat-free mayonnaise dressing or salad dressing

2 tablespoons fat-free milk

1 to 2 tablespoons stone-ground mustard or Dijon-style mustard

method

1 In a saucepan cook tortellini according to package directions, except stir in frozen peas and carrots along with tortellini. Drain.

2 In a large mixing bowl combine mayonnaise dressing or salad dressing, milk, and mustard. Add cooked tortellini and vegetables, stirring to coat.

3 Cover and refrigerate for at least 4 hours or up to 24 hours. Makes 4 main-dish servings.

To tote for lunch: Place 1 serving in an airtight container. Place in an insulated lunch box with a frozen ice pack.

Nutrition facts per serving:

259 calories, 5 g total fat (2 g saturated fat), 30 mg cholesterol, 714 mg sodium, 43 g carbohydrate, 2 g fiber, 12 g protein

Exchanges: 2½ Starch, 1 Vegetable, ½ Fat

dinners

success tips

Many diets tell you exactly what and when to eat, and seldom take into account your likes, dislikes, and lifestyle. No wonder diets don't work! Plan meals and snacks according to your own preferences and you'll be more successful in keeping the weight off.

Chicken Cacciatore (recipe on page 31)

chicken cacciatore

Preparation time: *25 minutes*   Cooking time: *20 minutes*

Cacciatore is Italian for "hunter" and usually contains mushrooms, tomatoes, onions, and herbs. If you like, replace the $1/4$ cup water with red wine, an optional ingredient often used in this classic dish *(pictured on page 30)*.

Nonstick cooking spray

4 small skinless, boneless chicken breast halves ($3/4$ pound total)

1 $14^1/2$-ounce can stewed tomatoes, undrained

1 medium green sweet pepper, cut into thin strips

$1/2$ cup sliced fresh mushrooms

$1/4$ cup chopped onion

$1/4$ cup water or dry red wine

2 teaspoons dried Italian seasoning, crushed

$1/8$ teaspoon ground black pepper

method

1 Coat an unheated large skillet with nonstick cooking spray. Preheat over medium heat. Add chicken and cook about 6 minutes or until lightly browned, turning to brown evenly.

2 Stir in undrained stewed tomatoes, sweet pepper, mushrooms, onion, water, Italian seasoning, and black pepper. Bring to boiling; reduce heat. Simmer, covered, about 15 minutes or until chicken is tender and no longer pink. Remove chicken from skillet; cover chicken to keep warm. Simmer tomato mixture, uncovered, about 5 minutes or to desired consistency. Serve over chicken. Makes 4 servings.

Nutrition facts per serving:

134 calories, 3 g total fat (1 g saturated fat), 45 mg cholesterol, 309 mg sodium, 10 g carbohydrate, 3 g fiber, 18 g protein

Exchanges: 2 Lean Meat, 2 Vegetable

barbecue-sauced beef sandwiches

Preparation time: *40 minutes*   Cooking time: *2 hours*

Serve half of these saucy sandwiches now and freeze the rest for later. When you're short on time, you'll have a ready-to-heat meal in the freezer.

1   2-pound boneless beef round steak, cut $^3/_4$ to 1 inch thick and trimmed of separable fat
    Nonstick spray coating
1   14$^1/_2$-ounce can tomatoes, undrained and cut up
1   cup chopped onion
1   cup chopped carrot
2   tablespoons Worcestershire sauce
2   tablespoons vinegar
1   tablespoon brown sugar
2   teaspoons chili powder
1   teaspoon dried oregano, crushed
$^1/_8$ teaspoon pepper
1   clove garlic, minced
1   bay leaf
8   hamburger buns, split and toasted

method

1 Cut meat into 4 to 6 pieces. Coat an unheated Dutch oven with nonstick cooking spray. Add half of the steak pieces; brown each piece on both sides. Remove meat. Repeat to brown remaining meat. Drain off fat. Return all meat to Dutch oven.

2 Add undrained tomatoes, onion, carrot, Worcestershire, vinegar, brown sugar, chili powder, oregano, pepper, garlic, and bay leaf. Bring to boiling; reduce heat. Simmer, covered, 2 to 2½ hours or until meat is tender.

3 Remove meat from sauce; shred meat. Return meat to sauce. If necessary, simmer, uncovered, for 5 to 10 minutes or until slightly thickened. Discard bay leaf. Serve in buns. Makes 8 servings.

Freezing Directions: Transfer mixture to freezer containers. Seal, label, and freeze for up to 6 months. To reheat, transfer mixture to a saucepan; add 1 tablespoon water. Cook, covered, over medium-low heat until heated through, stirring occasionally to break up. (Allow 8 to 10 minutes for 1 or 2 servings; 25 to 30 minutes for 4 servings.)

Nutrition facts per serving:
319 calories, 8 g total fat (2 g saturated fat), 72 mg cholesterol, 393 mg sodium, 30 g carbohydrate, 2 g fiber, 31 g protein

Exchanges: 2 Starch, 3 Lean Meat, 1 Vegetable

chicken and penne with basil sauce

Start to finish: *25 minutes*

If fresh basil is unavailable, do not substitute dried basil. Use another fresh herb instead, such as tarragon, thyme, or sage. Dried herbs just can't compare to the flavor of fresh herbs used here.

1¼ cups reduced-sodium chicken broth

4 teaspoons cornstarch

⅛ teaspoon ground black pepper

2 cups packaged dried penne pasta
   Nonstick cooking spray

1 medium red sweet pepper, cut into thin strips

1 medium yellow or green sweet pepper, cut into thin strips

3 cloves garlic, minced

1 tablespoon cooking oil

¾ pound skinless, boneless chicken breast halves, cut into 1-inch cubes

¼ cup lightly packed fresh basil leaves, cut into thin shreds

2 tablespoons shredded Parmesan cheese
   Fresh basil (optional)

method

1 Stir together chicken broth, cornstarch, and black pepper. Set aside.

2 Cook pasta according to package directions, omitting any oil and salt. Drain. Cover; keep warm.

3 Meanwhile, coat an unheated large skillet with nonstick cooking spray. Preheat over medium heat. Add sweet peppers and garlic. Stir-fry for 2 to 3 minutes or until sweet peppers are crisp-tender. Remove from skillet. Add the oil to skillet; increase heat to medium-high. Add chicken; stir-fry for 3 to 4 minutes or until chicken is no longer pink.

Stir broth mixture; add to skillet. Cook and stir until thickened and bubbly. Return sweet pepper mixture to skillet; add the ¼ cup basil shreds. Cook and stir for 2 minutes more. Toss with hot pasta. Sprinkle with Parmesan cheese. If desired, garnish with additional basil. Makes 4 servings.

Nutrition facts per serving:
330 calories, 8 g total fat (1 g saturated fat), 47 mg cholesterol, 282 mg sodium, 39 g carbohydrate, 1 g fiber, 24 g protein
Exchanges: 2 Starch, 2 Lean Meat, 2 Vegetable

beef with mushroom-tomato sauce

Preparation time: *20 minutes*   Grilling time: *10 minutes*

Serve up this dish when entertaining friends or on busy weeknights. It's quick and easy but deliciously satisfying. Cook a frozen vegetable blend and open a bagged salad mix and dinner is done.

1/8 teaspoon pepper

4 3-ounce beef eye of round steaks, trimmed of separable fat

1 cup sliced fresh mushrooms

1/2 cup sliced green onions

2 cloves garlic, minced

2 teaspoons margarine or butter

2 teaspoons cornstarch

2/3 cup no-salt-added vegetable juice

1/2 teaspoon instant beef bouillon granules

method

1 Rub pepper over meat. Place the meat on the unheated rack of a broiler pan. Broil 4 to 5 inches from the heat to desired doneness, turning once. [Allow 10 to 12 minutes for medium rare (145°) or 12 to 15 minutes for medium (160°).]

2 Meanwhile, in a saucepan cook mushrooms, green onions, and garlic in hot margarine or butter until vegetables are tender. Stir in cornstarch. Add vegetable juice and bouillon granules. Cook and stir until thickened. Cook and stir for 2 minutes more. Keep warm while cooking meat. Serve sauce over meat. Makes 4 servings.

Nutrition facts per serving:
173 calories, 8 g total fat (2 g saturated fat), 58 mg cholesterol, 172 mg sodium, 5 g carbohydrate, 0 g fiber, 20 g protein
Exchanges: 3 Lean Meat, 1 Vegetable

beef with red wine sauce 179 calories

Prepare as directed above, except substitute 1/3 cup dry red wine plus 1/3 cup water for the vegetable juice.

Nutrition facts per serving:
179 calories, 8 g total fat (2 g saturated fat), 58 mg cholesterol, 175 mg sodium, 3 g carbohydrate, 0 g fiber, 20 g protein
Exchanges: 3 Lean Meat, 1 Vegetable

baked chimichangas

Preparation time: *25 minutes*   Baking time: *15 minutes*

Use leftover roasted chicken or turkey or roast beef or pork for this Mexican favorite. Freeze any extra chimichangas for another meal (see directions, below).

1/2 pound cooked chicken, turkey, pork, or beef (1 1/2 cups)

1 16-ounce can fat-free refried beans

1 8-ounce jar salsa

1 4 1/2-ounce can diced green chili peppers, drained

3 tablespoons thinly sliced green onion

1 cup shredded reduced-fat Monterey Jack cheese or cheddar cheese (4 ounces)

8 8- to 9-inch flour tortillas
Fat-free dairy sour cream (optional)
Salsa (optional)
Thinly sliced green onion (optional)

method

1 Using 2 forks, shred cooked poultry, pork, or beef. In a large skillet combine poultry or meat, beans, the 8-ounce jar salsa, chili peppers, and the 3 tablespoons green onion. Cook and stir over medium heat until heated through. Stir in cheese.

2 Meanwhile, wrap the tortillas in foil; warm in a 350° oven for 10 minutes. For each chimichanga, spoon about 1/2 cup of the meat mixture onto a tortilla, near one edge. Fold in sides; roll up.

3 Place in a 13x9x2-inch baking pan. Bake, uncovered, in a 350° oven for 15 to 20 minutes or until heated through and tortillas are crisp and brown. If desired, serve with sour cream, additional salsa, and/or green onion. Makes 8 servings.

Freezing Directions: Place the unbaked chimichangas in freezer containers. Seal, label, and freeze for up to 6 months. To prepare, wrap the frozen chimichangas individually in foil. Bake in a 350° oven for 50 minutes. (Or, thaw chimichangas in refrigerator overnight. Wrap each in foil and bake about 30 minutes.) Remove the foil. Bake for 10 minutes more or until tortilla is crisp and brown.

Nutrition facts per serving:
258 calories, 9 g total fat (3 g saturated fat), 37 mg cholesterol, 685 mg sodium, 28 g carbohydrate, 3 g fiber, 18 g protein

Exchanges: 1 1/2 Starch, 2 Lean Meat, 1 Vegetable

pork roast with pineapple chutney

Preparation time: *15 minutes* Roasting time: *1¼ hours*
Standing time: *15 minutes*

To cook meat to perfection, always use a meat thermometer. When the thermometer reaches the correct temperature, push it in a little farther. If the temperature drops, continue cooking. If it stays the same, the roast is done.

- 1 2-pound boneless pork loin roast (single loin), trimmed of separable fat
- ¼ teaspoon ground black pepper
- 1 20-ounce can crushed pineapple (juice-pack), undrained
- ½ cup chopped onion
- 2 tablespoons raisins
- 2 tablespoons brown sugar
- 2 tablespoons vinegar
- 2 teaspoons grated fresh ginger or ½ teaspoon ground ginger
- ½ teaspoon ground cinnamon
- ⅛ teaspoon crushed red pepper (optional)
- Fresh herb sprigs (optional)

method

1 Rub pork with the black pepper. Place pork on a rack in a shallow roasting pan. Insert a meat thermometer into the pork. Roast, uncovered, in a 325° oven about 1¼ hours or until thermometer registers 155°. Cover; let stand 15 minutes (meat temperature will rise 5° during standing).

2 Meanwhile, for chutney, in a medium saucepan combine undrained pineapple, onion, raisins, brown sugar, vinegar, ginger, cinnamon, and crushed red pepper

(if desired). Bring to boiling; reduce heat. Simmer, uncovered, about 30 minutes or until liquid is syrupy. Serve warm with roast. If desired, garnish each serving with a sprig of fresh herb. Makes 8 servings.

Nutrition facts per serving:
199 calories, 7 g total fat (3 g saturated fat), 51 mg cholesterol, 42 mg sodium, 17 g carbohydrate, 1 g fiber, 17 g protein
Exchanges: 2 Lean Meat, 1 Fruit

bow ties and cheese

Preparation time: *20 minutes*   Baking time: *30 minutes*

Pasta ranks high among dieters because it's very filling. Serve this dish
with a simple vegetable, such as steamed broccoli or green beans,
or a fresh tossed salad drizzled with low-calorie dressing.

1 8-ounce package dried
  medium bow-tie pasta
1/4 cup finely chopped onion
2 teaspoons cooking oil
2 teaspoons all-purpose flour
1 teaspoon dry mustard
1/3 cup fat-free milk
1 cup fat-free cottage cheese

2/3 cup shredded reduced-fat
  cheddar cheese
  Nonstick cooking spray
1 tablespoon toasted wheat
  germ or fine dry bread crumbs
  Chopped tomato (optional)
  Sliced green onion (optional)

method

1 Cook pasta according to package
directions, except omit any oil.
2 In a large saucepan cook onion in
hot oil until tender. Stir in the flour
and mustard. Add milk all at once.
Cook and stir until thickened and
bubbly. Stir in the cottage cheese
and cheddar cheese. Cook and stir
over low heat until cheddar cheese
is melted. Stir in the drained pasta.
3 Coat a 1½-quart casserole with
nonstick cooking spray. Spoon
pasta mixture into casserole. Bake,
covered, in a 350° oven for

20 minutes. Uncover and sprinkle
with wheat germ or bread crumbs.
Bake, uncovered, for 10 to 15
minutes more or until heated
through. If desired, garnish with
tomato and green onion. Makes
5 servings.

Nutrition facts per serving:
296 calories, 6 g total fat (1 g saturated fat), 16 mg cholesterol,
301 mg sodium, 40 g carbohydrate,
0 g fiber, 19 g protein
Exchanges: 2½ Starch, 2 Lean Meat

citrus-tarragon salmon steaks

Preparation time: *20 minutes* Marinating time: *45 minutes*
Grilling time: *6 minutes*

Unlike meat and poultry, fish needs only a short time to marinate. In fact, acidic ingredients, such as citrus juices and vinegars, will cause fish to become tough and chewy with long marinating.

4 fresh or frozen salmon steaks, cut $3/4$ inch thick (about 1 pound)
1 teaspoon finely shredded orange peel
$1/4$ cup orange juice
$1/4$ cup lime juice
1 tablespoon champagne vinegar or white wine vinegar

1 tablespoon snipped fresh tarragon or $1/2$ teaspoon dried tarragon, crushed
1 teaspoon olive oil or cooking oil
$1/4$ teaspoon salt
$1/8$ teaspoon pepper
Nonstick cooking spray

method

1 Thaw salmon steaks, if frozen. Rinse fish; pat dry with paper towels. For the marinade, stir together the orange peel, orange juice, lime juice, vinegar, tarragon, oil, salt, and pepper.

2 Place fish in a shallow nonmetal baking dish. Pour marinade over fish. Cover and marinate in the refrigerator for 45 minutes, turning the fish once. Drain fish, reserving the marinade.

3 Coat an unheated grill rack with nonstick cooking spray. Grill fish on prepared rack over medium coals for 6 to 9 minutes or until fish just begins to flake easily when tested with a fork; turn the fish halfway through the grilling time and brush with reserved marinade. Makes 4 servings.

Nutrition facts per serving:
179 calories, 8 g total fat (1 g saturated fat), 42 mg cholesterol, 184 mg sodium, 4 g carbohydrate, 0 g fiber, 24 g protein
Exchanges: 3 Lean Meat

desserts

success tips

Make short-term and long-term weight goals. Write them down and keep track of your progress. Reward yourself for reaching each goal, but not with food. Treat yourself with a new pair of walking shoes, an outfit, or whatever makes you feel good and contributes to your overall health.

Lemon Dessert with Raspberries (recipe on page 41)

lemon dessert with raspberries

Preparation time: *30 minutes*   Chilling time: *4 hours*

This tart dessert combines cubes of angel food cake with lemon-spiked gelatin. The cool smoothness of the lemony gelatin is a perfect contrast to the light texture of the angel food cake *(pictured on page 40)*.

Nonstick cooking spray
1 4-serving-size package sugar-free lemon-flavored gelatin
$^1/_2$ cup boiling water
1 12-ounce can evaporated fat-free milk
$^1/_2$ of a 6-ounce can ($^1/_3$ cup) frozen lemonade concentrate, thawed
2 cups cubed angel food cake
2 cups fresh raspberries
1 tablespoon sugar

method

1 Coat the bottom of an 8-inch springform pan with cooking spray. Set aside.
2 In a large bowl dissolve the lemon gelatin in the boiling water. Stir in the evaporated fat-free milk and thawed lemonade concentrate. Cover and refrigerate until mixture mounds when spooned (1 to 1$^1/_2$ hours), stirring occasionally.
3 Beat the gelatin mixture with an electric mixer on medium to high speed for 5 to 6 minutes or until mixture is fluffy.
4 Arrange angel food cake cubes in the bottom of the prepared pan. Pour gelatin mixture over cake cubes. Cover and refrigerate for at least 4 hours or until firm.

5 Meanwhile, in a small bowl stir together the raspberries and sugar. Cover and refrigerate for at least 2 hours.
6 To serve, remove side of pan. Cut dessert into wedges; place on dessert plates. Top each serving with raspberries. Makes 12 servings.

Nutrition facts per serving:
89 calories, 0 g total fat, 1 mg cholesterol, 107 mg sodium, 18 g carbohydrate, 1 g fiber, 4 g protein
Exchanges: 1 Starch

chocolate-cinnamon angel cake

Preparation time: *50 minutes*   Baking time: *40 minutes*

A mild chocolate flavor accented with cinnamon sets this angel cake apart
from others. However, it's still low in calories and fat free.
Chocolate purists can omit the cinnamon.

1½ cups egg whites
(10 to 12 large egg whites)
1½ cups sifted powdered sugar
1 cup sifted cake flour or sifted
all-purpose flour
3 tablespoons unsweetened
cocoa powder

¼ teaspoon ground cinnamon
1½ teaspoons cream of tartar
1 teaspoon vanilla
1 cup granulated sugar
Chocolate-flavored syrup
(optional)

method

1 Allow egg whites to stand at room temperature for 30 minutes.
2 Meanwhile, sift powdered sugar, flour, cocoa powder, and cinnamon together 3 times. Set aside.
3 In a large mixing bowl combine the egg whites, cream of tartar, and vanilla; beat with an electric mixer on medium speed until soft peaks form (tips curl).
4 Gradually add the granulated sugar, about 2 tablespoons at a time, beating on high speed until stiff peaks form (tips stand straight). If bowl is too full, transfer to a larger bowl.
5 Sift about one-fourth of the flour mixture over the beaten egg whites; fold in gently. Repeat, folding in the remaining flour

mixture by fourths. Pour into an ungreased 10-inch tube pan. Using a narrow metal spatula or knife, gently cut through the batter to eliminate any air bubbles.
6 Bake on the lowest rack in a 350° oven for 40 to 45 minutes or until top springs back when lightly touched.
7 Immediately invert cake (leave in pan); cool completely. Loosen side of cake from pan; remove cake. If desired, serve cake slices drizzled with chocolate-flavored syrup. Makes 16 servings.

Nutrition facts per serving:
125 calories, 0 g total fat, 0 mg cholesterol, 35 mg sodium, 28 g carbohydrate, 0 g fiber, 3 g protein
Exchanges: 1½ Starch

bread pudding

Preparation time: *15 minutes*   Baking time: *35 minutes*   Cooling time: *20 minutes*

If you like, top warm bowls of this homespun dessert with fresh, frozen, or canned fruit.
Or, serve it with vanilla-flavored fat-free frozen yogurt (adds 120 calories per half cup).

Nonstick cooking spray
2 eggs
2 egg whites
1¹/₂ cups fat-free milk
2 tablespoons honey

1 teaspoon vanilla
3 cups cubed raisin bread
  (4 to 5 slices)
  Orange sections (optional)

method

1 Coat a 9-inch pie plate with cooking spray. Set aside.
2 In a large mixing bowl beat together the eggs and egg whites until combined. Beat in the milk, honey, and vanilla. Stir in the bread cubes. Pour into the prepared pie plate.
3 Bake bread pudding in a 325° oven for 35 to 40 minutes or until puffed and a knife inserted near the center comes out clean.

Let stand at room temperature about 20 minutes to cool slightly before serving. If desired, garnish with orange sections. Makes 6 servings.

Nutrition facts per serving:
124 calories, 3 g total fat (1 g saturated fat), 72 mg cholesterol, 139 mg sodium, 18 g carbohydrate, 0 g fiber, 7 g protein
Exchanges: 1 Starch, ½ Milk

frozen cranberry pie

Preparation time: *20 minutes*   Freezing time: *4 hours*

To soften the ice cream, place it in a chilled bowl and stir with a wooden spoon just until it is soft enough to stir in the remaining ingredients. If the ice cream becomes too soft, the pie will be icy instead of creamy.

Nonstick cooking spray
6 chocolate wafer cookies, finely crushed (about ¹/₃ cup)
1 quart vanilla low-fat or light ice cream

1 cup whole-berry cranberry sauce
1 teaspoon finely shredded orange peel
  Sugared cranberries (optional)*

method

1 Coat a 9-inch pie plate with cooking spray. Coat with the crushed cookies. Set aside.
2 In a chilled medium mixing bowl stir the ice cream with a wooden spoon just until softened. Fold in the cranberry sauce and orange peel until combined. Spoon mixture into prepared pie plate. Cover and freeze for at least 4 hours or until firm.

3 To serve, cut into wedges. If desired, garnish with sugared cranberries. Makes 8 servings.
*Note: To make sugared cranberries, roll frozen cranberries in sugar.

Nutrition facts per serving:
176 calories, 3 g total fat (1 g saturated fat), 11 mg cholesterol, 83 mg sodium, 36 g carbohydrate, 1 g fiber, 2 g protein
Exchanges: 1 Starch, 1 Fruit, ½ Fat

snacks

success tips

Listen and trust your body's signals of hunger and fullness. Make sure you're not eating for emotional reasons—boredom, anger, or loneliness. When mealtime arrives, take time to really enjoy your food. Concentrate on tasting all of the flavors in your meal. It takes about 20 minutes for your stomach to tell your brain that you're full. So slower is better when you're trying not to overeat.

Layered Bean Dip (recipe on page 45)

layered bean dip

Preparation time: *25 minutes*   Chilling time: *2 to 24 hours*

Ounce for ounce, our homemade Tortilla Crisps have one-third fewer calories than fried corn tortilla chips and much less fat, too *(pictured on page 44)*.

- 1 15-ounce can pinto or red kidney beans, drained
- 1/4 cup purchased salsa
- 1 4 1/2-ounce can diced green chili peppers, drained
- 4 ounces bottled roasted red sweet peppers or one 4-ounce jar pimientos, drained and chopped (about 1/2 cup)

- 1 cup low-fat cottage cheese
- 1 cup chopped tomato
- 1/4 cup sliced green onions
- 1/4 cup shredded reduced-fat cheddar cheese
- 1 recipe Tortilla Crisps (recipe below) or assorted vegetable dippers

method

1 In a food processor bowl or blender container place beans and salsa. Cover and blend or process until smooth. Spread mixture evenly in a shallow bowl or a 9-inch pie plate. Top with chili peppers and roasted red peppers or pimientos.

2 Wash food processor bowl or blender container. Place cottage cheese in the food processor bowl or blender container. Cover and process or blend until smooth. Spread cottage cheese on top of peppers in bowl or pie plate. Cover; refrigerate for at least 2 hours or up to 24 hours.

3 To serve, sprinkle tomato, green onions, and cheddar cheese over dip. Serve with Tortilla Crisps or assorted fresh vegetables. Makes 18 (1/4-cup) servings.

Tortilla Crisps: Cut twelve 6-inch flour or corn tortillas into 6 wedges each. Place wedges in a single layer on an ungreased baking sheet. Bake the tortillas in batches in a 350° oven for 8 to 10 minutes or until crisp.

Nutrition facts per 1/4 cup dip and 4 Tortilla Crisps: 81 calories, 2 g total fat (1 g saturated fat), 2 mg cholesterol, 185 mg sodium, 12 g carbohydrate, 2 g fiber, 5 g protein
Exchanges: 1/2 Starch, 1 Vegetable

sugar and spice popcorn

Preparation time: *15 minutes* Baking time: *15 minutes*
Cooling time: *30 minutes*

Plain air-popped popcorn is the recommended choice for dieters.
But why eat that flavorless stuff when you can enjoy this version
spiced with cinnamon, nutmeg, and ginger?

Nonstick cooking spray
6 cups popped popcorn
(using no oil)
2 tablespoons sugar

2 teaspoons water
¼ teaspoon ground cinnamon
⅛ teaspoon ground nutmeg
⅛ teaspoon ground ginger

method

1 Coat a 13x9x2-inch baking pan
with nonstick cooking spray. Place
popcorn in the pan.
2 In a small mixing bowl stir together
sugar, water, cinnamon, nutmeg, and
ginger. Drizzle spice mixture over
popcorn in baking pan. Toss
popcorn until coated. Bake in a
350° oven for 15 minutes, stirring
once or twice.
3 Transfer the hot popcorn from
baking pan to a large piece of foil.
Cool popcorn completely. Store
leftovers in a tightly covered
storage container. Makes 8
(¾-cup) servings.

Nutrition facts per serving:
32 calories, 0 g total fat, 0 mg
cholesterol, 0 mg sodium, 7 g
carbohydrate, 0 g fiber, 1 g protein
Exchanges: ½ Starch

biscotti

Preparation time: *25 minutes* Baking time: *31 minutes*
Cooling time: *2 hours*

A specialty of coffeehouses, these twice-baked Italian cookies make a great ending to any meal. With fewer than 40 calories each, they can curb your sweet tooth without causing you pangs of guilt.

Nonstick cooking spray
2 cups all-purpose flour
2 teaspoons baking powder
2 teaspoons anise seed, crushed

1 teaspoon finely shredded
 lemon peel
1/4 cup butter
1/2 cup sugar
2 eggs

method

1 Coat a large cookie sheet with cooking spray. Set aside.
2 In a medium mixing bowl stir together the flour, baking powder, anise seed, and lemon peel. Set flour mixture aside.
3 In a small mixing bowl beat butter with an electric mixer on medium speed for 30 seconds. Add sugar; beat until combined. Add eggs; beat well. Stir in flour mixture.

4 On waxed paper, shape dough into two 12-inch-long logs. Place logs on prepared cookie sheet; flatten logs slightly.
5 Bake logs in a 375° oven for 15 to 20 minutes or until lightly browned. Cool completely on wire racks (about 1 hour).
6 Cut each log into ½-inch-thick slices. Arrange slices, cut sides down, on the baking sheet.
7 Bake in a 325° oven for 8 minutes. Turn over. Bake 8 to 10 minutes more or until crisp and light brown. Transfer to wire racks and cool completely. Makes 48 cookies.

Nutrition facts per cookie:
38 calories, 1 g total fat (1 g saturated fat), 12 mg cholesterol, 29 mg sodium, 6 g carbohydrate, 0 g fiber, 1 g protein
Exchanges: ½ Starch

mocha milk shakes

Start to finish: *10 minutes*

Even adults swoon for a milk shake. This variation takes a childhood-favorite drink and gives it grown-up appeal with a hint of coffee flavor.

2 cups chocolate low-fat
    frozen yogurt
$1/2$ cup fat-free milk

2 to 3 teaspoons instant
    coffee crystals

method

1 Place frozen yogurt, milk, and coffee crystals in a blender container. Cover and blend until smooth. Serve immediately. Makes 2 (8-ounce) servings.

Nutrition facts per serving:
    186 calories, 3 g total fat (2 g saturated fat), 21 mg cholesterol, 163 mg sodium, 36 g carbohydrate, 0 g fiber, 8 g protein
Exchanges: 2 Starch, ½ Milk

tropical banana milk shakes 95 calories

Choose a low-fat ice cream for this blended shake to keep the fat and calories under control. As a midafternoon snack, share it with your kids and feel good about it being good for them, too.
  1 small banana
  1 cup orange juice
  1 cup vanilla low-fat
    or light ice cream
$1/4$ teaspoon vanilla
    Ground nutmeg
    Orange slices, halved
    (optional)
    Orange peel strips (optional)

1 Peel and cut up banana. Place in freezer container or bag; freeze until firm.
2 In a blender container combine banana, orange juice, ice cream, and vanilla. Cover and blend until smooth. Sprinkle each serving with nutmeg. If desired, garnish with orange slice halves and orange peel strips. Makes 4 (6-ounce) servings.
Nutrition facts per serving:
    95 calories, 2 g total fat (1 g saturated fat), 5 mg cholesterol, 29 mg sodium, 19 g carbohydrate, 1 g fiber, 2 g protein
Exchanges: ½ Fruit, ½ Milk